Martin Boronte was born in south London ir for his 16-page work that he penned back in in remember now what it was about (the manuscript, he contained a lot of big words – as in their physical size – and that some of them spilled onto the desk. This, then, is his much better contained, and long-awaited, second book. He continues to live in London.

Important Celebrity Reviews

These will *surely* be coming in their throngs soon, consequently the rest of this page has been kept as blnk* as poss** in order to rec*** them in future editions.

––––––––––

*Blank.
**Possible.
***Receive, record and/or recognise.

I Mean It, Daphne!

MARTIN BORONTE

First published in paperback in 2020
by Amazon Publishing

ISBN 978 1 9163526 1 2

www.martinboronte.com
www.imeanitdaphne.com

For my (fantastic) parents Daphne & Peter

C⊗NTENTS

ACKNOWLEDGEMENTS

Thank you to my amazing wife, Eleni, for putting up with yet another extremely elaborate attempt by me to appear busy.

Rob Gibbons, Neil Gibbons and Steve Coogan for their inspiring book, *Alan Partridge: Nomad*.

Heathrow Airport for finding and returning to me my lost phone, on which I had made a load of notes for this book, and never wasted time on it by mindlessly swiping away at multicoloured candy like a mad man (because I have an iPad for that).

Finally, thanks to leftfield UK piano trio GoGo Penguin for providing me with the majority of background music while I was writing this book, most notably their albums Man Made Object and A Humdrum Star.

PREFACE

This is my dad, Peter. While he's not around anymore, he would've been very pleased to meet you!

Peter was Hungarian and a man of quite wise words. 'Only speak vhen you've got someting to say, Martin' was one such Platoesque, albeit slightly mispronounced, offering – advice which, decades on, I still stick to, to a fault. But now I *do* have something to say, hence this unusually chatty effort.

Some pearls of Mr Boronte's wisdom, however, weren't to be relied on or recommended in any way – such as our family being related to the Brontë sisters *and* Attila the Hun (even if that improbable combo explains the romantic, yet aggressive, nature of this book, which is bursting with childish humour), and swearing to step into the mouth of anyone who annoyed him, and shit himself. Of course, that particular gem might be a classic one-liner or tradition where he came from but in this country it's bordering on, if not horribly overstepping, the offensive. Regardless, he had a hugely positive influence on me, which is why I'm introducing you to him like this, twenty years on from when he signed off.

The expression 'I mean it, Daphne!' is what dad would shout a lot, often in response to something on television that he didn't like or agree with, and which served as a forewarning to Daphne – the vonderful vife – of a subsequent volley of vulgarities. The venue of these Hungarian harangues was usually the front room, although I can't swear to that, like dad could, because he and the room were habitually shrouded in fag smoke. His actual whereabouts during these TV episodes was revealed by the illuminated and droopy end of a self-rolled cigarette piercing the gloom, or by the sudden sound of a weighty 1970s glass ashtray smashing into things.

Anyway, his smoking addiction, sadly, cut short his impassioned and worthy attempts at setting the world to rights, which is, naturally, where

1

I step in …not to shit myself, I must add, but to write this book. And if I'm half as entertaining as dad, which, according to DNA, I am, then it'll be as though he's only gone away just fractionally.

Daphne, by the way, is still doing pretty well, as can be seen in the lifelike self-drawn illustration on page 197 (by me, not her – she's atrocious at drawing), having shrewdly steered clear of cigs for much of her life, as well as flying receptacles for them.

Tank you, son.

P.S. Despite pointing out my dad's filty language, as in colourful, I've decided it best to keep swear words to a minimum throughout – partly for brevity but mainly to appeal to those with more rounded vocabularies.

PEPLE

Extraordinary earthbound beings weighed down only by stupidity

Thesaurus
British, inflated, non-binary, gifted, chatty, insecure, poser, blatherer, ignorant, shy, character, deluded, intrusive, smelly, boastful, atishoo, happy, thoughtfull, wannabe, American, pompous, Aussie, impatient, shopaholic, gorilla, angry, apathetic obese, chav

In that order then…

Don't Mention The Flaw

They say that British people are an unfriendly and snobby lot, who are always apologising for stuff. We're sorry, but we strongly disagree with that very foreign assumption. And who are "they" anyhow – they need to piss right off!*.

Yes, stereotyping might be a neat way to label a nation, but it can also be upsetting – like going to the dentist, losing an umbrella or running out of tea. Thank goodness, then, for our stiff upper lip and for our long history of being able to deal with such passive aggression, which, fortunately, has equipped us with the ability to hold on to our innate superiority in the face of such tumult …and, thankfully, to our bowler hats.

---

*Some good old British sarcasm** there.
**A synonym (in Britain) for comedy gold.

Beach Balls

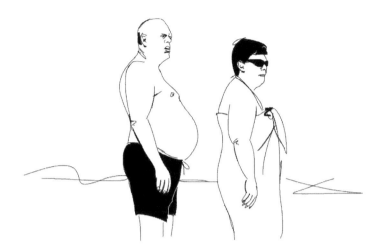

Middle-aged guys with not an ounce of flat on them, wowing the ladies with their ultra-unsound bulges.

We have to hand it to them* – they look like they're expecting a pumped up beach ball at any minute, with their middle wives beside them, but not that they care. They're too busy inflating their opinion of themselves, while swaggering across breaking waters and avoiding toppling over.

Fat shaming aside, at least they've managed to lose the tracksuit livery – if not, regrettably, the suit tracks.

By the way, it was a toy.

---

*Another beer and doughnut?

Boys And Girls And Noise And Twirls

It's not that we don't appreciate that some people prefer to assign themselves as gender neutral, or non-binary, rather than good old* male or female …or that identifying oneself as a boy or girl these days can be confusing, especially if we're into anime and never look down …or how difficult it is choosing a baby's name, so why not just call it *theyby* for now, and let them self-identify their own preferred gender – and, while they're at it, also pick which university they want to go to.

Obviously not. It's just the supreme smug superiority and faddishness of it all – matched only, right now, by that other unnatural assemblage of attention-seeking pseudo-humans …vegans, which just makes us want to slap/punch** them in the face. That's all.

---

*Four billion years old.

**Depending on their perceived gender.

A Star

School (sku:l) *n* – a place where instruction is given to young people, unless we're a gifted and annoying know-it-all with an oversized brain, in which case, we knew that already, but we'll turn up anyway for the laugh, and to make ourselves known to the teachers.

Such boy and girl automatons of knowledge may be unfazed by simple things, like facts, and are the pride of any school*, but there are things for which, if they're not careful, they'll be marked down on. Like forming smug, arc-shaped, grins in the face of complex maths and straight-faced mates; raising hands in anticipation of questions; failing to assist the teachers; tutting at troublemakers; and being wholly unreceptive to justifiable jealous rage.

---

*And genius-lusting parent.

Dear Diarrhoea

Please help. I'm at my wits' end.

As someone with a regular vowel movement, how do I easily extricate myself from the relentless grip of people who've got the verbal shits?

I've tried most things, including, in order of meanness, listening, interrupting, zoning out, psychokinesis, faking incoming calls, pointing behind them, looking at my watch, looking bored, yawning, edging away, running away, putting my hand to their face, waving goodbye, being extremely rude, gaffer taping their mouth and throwing up all over them. All, alas, to no avail.

Hoping to hear from you soon … but do keep it short, thanks.

Serenity Moore

Knife Crime

Face facts – it's the forward-looking and, for some of us, ugly part of our heads that slowly sags with age. But that doesn't stop some of us backward-looking people, usually in the prime of our knife, searching for former facial fortunes, and even new ones altogether, as if our knives depended on it. But knife can be cruel, and results are rarely knife changing for the better.

Fortunately, a chance of a lifetime exists with a few simple and familiar operations of the neck muscles, whereupon our heads and faces can be lifted in an entirely free and natural way, to instantly create that elusive new lease of knlife.

Water Stunt

Rhyming slang aside, just when we thought it was safe to go on holiday with our daughter, a great white appears, prowling the coastline with its lifeless black eyes and golden teeth, and terrorising us with intermittent spurts of seawater, smugness and ambiguous stability.

What we are dealing with here is a perfect specimen, a competing machine. It's really a debacle of evolution. All this machine does is grin and overheat and make little farts, and that's all. Bad fish.

Here's to swimmin' without toe-webbed cretins.

Brainless Small Talk Costs Lives

'Hello, how are you?'
'I'm good, you?'
'Good-good, I'm good too.'
'Good. Good.'
'Good-good.'

Churchillianesque chat concluded, we can now focus on much more important matters. It seems that within the past few seconds of stiff stuffed silence, a bad foreign swine has masterminded an impolite and apocalyptic attack on our stores. We must strike back immediately. But before that, we will need to check on the weather.

'It's not bad today, isn't it.'
'Yes, it's much warmer than yesterday.'
'Yeah, it was absolutely bitter, wasn't it.'
'Bitter's not the word.'
'Terribly bitter it was.'

Terrible-terrible.

All Ears, No Listen, Dumbo

Listening is easy – it's the hearing that's the tricky bit. Or it might be the other way around, who knows.

Probably when we listened to/heard that juicy bit of aural, or is it oral, info, we were too busy with own thoughts, and everybody knows – even non-listeners – that it's impossible to keep tabs on more than one person talking at once.

So the next time we're in conversation, or getting directions to some-where as the elephant flies, and we find ourselves drifting off like this …say, at the thought of a scary mouse, who might easily scurry up our big ears if we're not careful, hence the need to consciously remember to prick them back …we just need to give people our full attention, and concentrate.

The first circus tent on the left.

Tongue Tied On A Bed Of Buttoned-Up Mushrooms

It's faulty gourmet night and we've been served up a plate of raw rat and gone off walnuts by blumen mistake. Normally, we don't hestontate to complain about oversights such as this but in restaurants, strangely, our table manners always seems to get the better of us. Now, we've limited ourselves to three choices of duck – done, of course, in three extremely different ways:

1. Duck the problem altogether. Who knows, rat might taste like cod.
2. Duck under the table with said rat and serve to the cat.
3. Duck surprise. Feign a sudden heart attack.

Sorry to say it, but ducking's off.

Old Age Tension

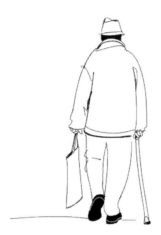

We've just bought our first ever lottery ticket, and we're in a rush to get home to celebrate, what's bound to be, our life-changing good fortune. Unfortunately, there's an elderly person in front of us, hogging the pavement and walking at a speed only tortoises and the old welcome. So, do we:

a) Cash in as soon as possible by making a youthful 'beep-beep' noise and agile undertaking manoeuvre?
b) Out of respect for their greater age and patience, hang back and defer our winnings until at least tomorrow?
c) Secretly tuck our (likely winning) lottery ticket into their bag?

Answer: As a society, we do all the above …whereas for individuals – like all of us – that, of course, is just another lottery.

The Name's Bond

Misclaims Bond. Licensed to act cool, despite all the quintessential sophistication of an imbecile who, because of extremely weak legs, leans on things a lot. But there's more to this real-life character than meets his diabolical, villainous and permanently squinting eye.

Not least the rebellious streak ...*he once stole a Finger of Fudge bar from a newsagent*; the signature drink ...*lager top with ice galore**; the cars ...*back-firing Ford Fiesta (Q reg)*; the thwarting of evil plots ...*multiple fag packets jettisoned into allotments*; the intelligence ...*lives life on a doesn't need to know basis*; the looks ...*like someone's just farted*; the gadgets ...*self-importance and arrogance*; the girls ...*mum*; the chase scenes ...*from the newsagent and allotment*; the weapons ...*hotshot at making moronic gun-shapes with hands*; the assignments ...*does the odd job of delivering papers and insults*.

Very much *mistaken*, not stirred.

---

*Pussy.

Surprise Surprise

It hits us right between the eyes. We're under ambush by unannounced guests!

Cue inevitable alarm, hostility and tightened fists (on our part) transitioned rapidly into fairly realistic-looking happiness and affection. Of course, our friends/family – the intruders – have never spotted that we're not the sort for surprising, so they certainly won't have detected any of our underlying terror and aggression, either, as a result of their sudden appearance, including a number of overly long stares at a red-stained shovel, which we keep handy for such "special" occasions.

'Oh, don't worry, we're not stopping.'

Thwang! …too late.

Welcome Tail Wind

Rectal tremor. Trouser cough. Cut a stinker.

Whichever delicate way we choose to describe it, farting is as natural as gas light and should not be frowned upon*, or indeed lit**.

Sadly, though, farting isn't for everyone, in spite of its lingering reminder that no matter how advanced we think we've become, our animal ways will forever trump and stick its nose up at our odorous, human, cheek.

---

*Unless it's one of those putrid puffs, upon which frown away and immediately seek shelter.
**Unless we've reached the televised stage of a talent show.

The Humblebrag

Are we humble? Or are we chancer?

I'm a bit annoyed with myself for taking so long to come up with that *Killer* opening line*, but looking for the answer to the questions, we are, quite often, both at the same time – which spells trouble, because modest show offs are more annoying than the lyrics to that song …if such a thing was possible.

The trick, which is instantly spotted for its lyric-like artificiality, involves boasting with humility in order to elicit equal amounts of adoration and affection – an endeavour that, if it wasn't for our amazing capacity to astound with delusions of grandeur (and sincerity), and to repeat the refrain, is as unbearable to endure as that song.

---

*An example of a humblebrag, which took forever to write because I'm in the middle of replying to fan mail**.
**Another lovely example of a humblebrag …and so forth.

Flower Cower

'Earth laughs in flowers'.

Either the author of that line, Ralph Waldo Emerson, was a former florist* or he was blatantly mocking the several hundred million people who are afflicted with the far from funny, ha-ha, hay fever. Who nose?

Otherwise, how else do we explain why, on one hand, nature gives us the most beautifully scented and delicate blossoms imaginable but, on the other, doesn't allow all of us to enjoy them without first having to stuff a deep-sea helmet on our heads and Vaseline up our nasal portholes (in reverse order), else losing our sense of smell and will to live because we're drowning in two fathoms of nostril waste.

---

*Or bee.

Perky Of The Job

The deadline is today. But the computer's not well, the printer's not speaking to paper, it's no-phones Friday, there's no milk again and someone's spilt (black) tea over Wendy*. For most working folk, this would be cause for considerable despair and booting of computers, particularly in view of the recurring milk disaster.

Step forward perpetually-perky Patrick, who, despite his charming cheeriness from birth, is obviously here just to make things even worse. Because, unless his daily routine begins with an early wake-up call from Lottery Head office, followed by some carefree computer hacking and a milk bath, then now's not the time for groundless grinning. That's saved for no-work Saturdays.

---

*The weeping fig.

I Think Therefore I Clam

The splendid art of thinking may have got us all to where we are today – reading this brief, but thoughtful, theory on thinking – but its common practise is thought of much too highly.

Think about it, when we don't think the best things seem to happen to us. Like finally being able to paint like a child, whose genius mind is uncluttered with mindless and damaging thinking …a Picasso aspiration; or like being able to play our best football when we're not thinking about it …by way of a Zidane gyration; or like having blood circulated by our non-thinking bodies to enable us to, hopefully, in due course, turn this important page …on our ponderous inner narration.

15 Minutes Of Drain

As the late, great, David Bowie once said, 'fame puts you there where things are hollow' – 'somewhere, for example, like a sewer outflow' …a potential follow-up line in that song, which, no doubt, because it's so badly written and its rhyming attributes stink, Bowie didn't go for.

But perhaps he should have, as it perfectly describes the world we live in, where, they say, at any given moment, we're never more than six feet away from a dirty and opportunistic rat face who's fallen into the trap of wanting to be famous – a common lyric plagued, inevitably, by funky regret that'll definitely be hard to swallow.

Confidence Trick

Next up, we have an American magician – just one of 330 million in America* alone – whose trick, which we've all seen before, is to routinely appear confident before our very eyes, regardless of the stage or scene. This is more than just an illusion, it's true wizardry. By contrast, us Brits have all the usual confidence of a magician's rabbit caught in the headlights of a village talent show.

Their secret? It lies in the their stage presence and flourish from birth, where the black art of instilling into every child the idea that you can, and will, succeed at anything, works like a magic wand. The big worry, of course, is if they try to palm it off onto us, as they do with most things, which will not only make us hopping mad but also, magically, cause our blushes** to appear.

---

*Population: 330 million.

**If not our twitching noses and big ears.

Billionaires Crow

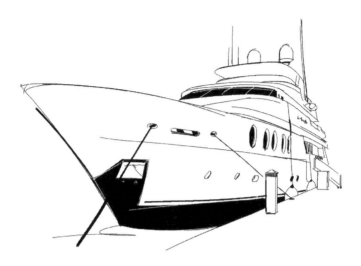

It's all self, self, self nowadays, especially if we're a blustering billionaire, whose wealth seems to accumulate around the brain, like lard, where the ego is found. Not mentioning individual names, but the Elon Bransons, the Vladimir Zuckerbergs and the Donald Bezoses of this world know who they are and, notably, so do we – because there's nothing they've all put more time, effort and money into achieving than just that.

So the next time we find ourselves on the receiving end of an inflating, self-congratulatory, balloon trip, or a rocketing, self-important, space trip, or a serving, self-serving, presidential trip, we should bring them down to earth for what, and who, they are – PR stunts*, with considerable self-worth, but which is balanced with billions in the red in self-respect.

---

*Rhymes with.

Uptalking On The Rise

It's one of modern life's most unsettling, yet grammatically admissible, questions – that of why spoken English has been slowly turned upside down in recent years, i.e. why are we all now speaking with highly questionable, pseudo-Aussie, up-inflections, where even the most banal remarks about Sheila and her flannie terminate in heaps of pipe-puffing, bum-prodding, tones of inquisitiveness?

Strewth, who knows mate??

Instead of blaming it all on our distant Neighbours, though, perhaps the answer lies much closer to home …with social media, where seeking to gain questionable attention and approval for anything that's *unquestionably* mundane is defo fair dinkum, Bruce???

Panic On The Seats

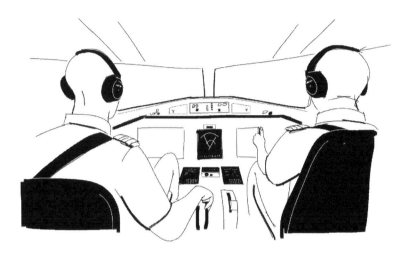

PILOT ALERT-PILOT ALERT

In the likely event that, upon landing, a retard passenger unfastens their seat belt before your say so, like the last sperm left on the shelf, then we recommend the following spoiler manoeuvres:

1. Turn on 'Belt up or die in a horrible ball of flames' sign
2. At the first hint of overhead bin enthusiasm, engage full reverse thrusters and prepare for passenger landings. Kangaroo braking may also be used, which is just as entertaining.
3. Spray pests liberally with insecticide, or with even more noxious inflight perfume
4. Retain luggage for subsequent high altitude release
5. Shove the lemmings off the plane without the jetty in place

Finally, thank them for flying baa-aa Airways.

How The West Is One

If only the stars would align so that we could use our unique collection of star stuff material to spend precious atomic energy buying utterly worthless and impotent collections of tsar stuff, like extravagant televisions and extra-vacant handbags.

Perhaps there should be a new universal law that states that material possessions may only be made from material, as in fabric – thus restricting our wanton western greed to *actual* necessities …like clothing, window dressings and things that make us feel warm and cosy at night.

D'oh!

Gorillas In Our Midst

The great ape. Also known as the self-important politician, or Guy, the big stocky bloke down the pub who lifts weights before pints, and is partial to admiring applause, therefore, whenever exiting said pub.

In their natural habitat these apes are easy to spot. The foraging for compliments, as mentioned, the ritualistic intimidatory charges, the grunts and/or flatulence, and, consequently, the scarce mating opportunities – are all a part of what's become legendary in the territory of heavyweight posturing.

But what sets these apes apart, from your standard ape, is the way they walk – with arms splayed out and rear-facing palms. Admittedly, while such armery comes in handy for blocking excitable troops of kids down alleyways, its more calculating and evolutionary function is to increase locomotory drag and so thereby afford themselves greater time in the spotlight. *A-ha*! Ape not so dumb after all.

Angry Grains Of Sand

The chance that we're here at all – living on a planet paradise that supports complex life, at this time in our universe, where not only have all our ancestors have had to come to be but also come together to produce us – is both comically and chemically astronomical. Lucky is not the word. *Implausible* is.

Yet even more mystifying, then, is how nature also conspires to yield some incredibly less-than-fortunate people, whose lives on this wonderland are blighted by continual anger. Such as the manager of a ridiculously blissful, beach-fronted, Seychellean restaurant, who I recently had the bad luck to get burnt by*, merely by converging with him on what was, he thought, his special time and place in the sand.

---

*Although I had been warned of old face-ache's existence, so I guess I only had myself – and the planet, the universe, and their long duplicitous histories – to blame.

Can't Be Asked

I don't know about you but I just don't have the energy or motivation lately to be bothered with all the general apathy that's going around. That may sound indifferent and unfeeling (and corny), but if the spiral of human, progress-ending, inaction like this is caused by "easylifeitus", as is likely, rather than underlying, non-lying, health issues, then why should we be sufficiently concerned to take action on it?

Regardless, please take it upon yourselves to take meaningful action now and, like someone who gives a toss, write your answer below – then return it to me, by hand, on a postcard, at your earliest convenience. The best solution, drawn out of a hat, might just save the world.

– – – –   – – –

Note: Rudeness above will not be tolerated. Unlike apathy.

Fat's Fair

It's been on most of our lips ever since the spread of fast food – no, not cheesy puffs, they, sadly, weren't invented back then – it's the query why those of us with big bones* aren't made to pay more for the imprint of our bulky backsides, like when we're being hauled around on buses and planes, or when taking up both seats four and five at Weight Watchers Live?

Perhaps bigger people like us should be charged by the amount of seat spillage, with humungously fat discounts applied to any adjacent seat space. It's likely such measures would appeal to slim folks who are intolerant to luminous orange snacks, for example, and value their health. Who knows, it might even be the start of a whole new sizeable relationship.

---

*Salad dodgers, fatsos, heffalumps, Two-Ton Tessies, cheesy puff addicts, etc.

Vacancy

Gav
19b Lower Class Way, Scallywag Town
Tel: Try 020 8588 3200
Mob: Latest Samsung
Email: gav19@supbruv.com

Profile

Gav is an aggressive and uncultured lout with extensive practice in antisocial behaviour and the start-up fights business. He is well versed in publicly fondling his testes, sneering at people, shoplifting and pushing drugs and quad pushchairs. Gav has first-hand experience in successful fake running wear, adopting the showy brand of arrogance of an orangutan. His experience includes working with the police and having underage sex.

Although Gav is a toothless cretin with poor taste, who sets terribly low standards of himself, which he propa achieves, innit, he is considered one of the most sorted chavs around town.

Experience

January 21st, 2020, 7.30am to 8.30am: Crew Member, McDonald's.

Education

There 'aint nuffink wot he don't know, bro.

Achievements

Had four kids before turning 18. Got a snooker table-sized TV, which he's been on nine times (Jeremy Kyle). Speaks mock English, Jamaican and New York. Owns more gold than H. Samuel.

ENTERTAINMENT & SPORT

Ready, camera, dissatisfaction

Thesaurus

shiny, mimey, artificial, served, breakfast, mate, acting, social, cinema,
celebrity, thwack, blackhole, sweat, blind, biased, testosterone, trace,
unbelievable, referee, abungle, patronise, dumbbell, blurry, Warhol,
fastest, elevenses, beanstalk, quiz, erotica, commentary, Netflix

Benz Meanz Shinez

- Shiny old car being held up bin lorry
- Dusty dirt track
- June 3rd, 1954 (bin collection day)

No matter the mode of transport, terrain or circumstances, just what is it with old vehicles, used in period films and TV programmes, always looking pristine, like they've just plopped off the end of the original production line, slippery soap-style?

Either the owners are charging the producers by the dust particle or everyone back in those days didn't dare risk going out in their vehicles …for fear of missing the bin men.

Lip Stync

Mime, mime a song
Mime out loud
Mime out strong
Mime of good things not bad
Mime of happy not sad

Those, the pretend lyrics of The Carpenters. Talking of which, I wonder if *actual* carpenters use pretend screws when feigning to hang imaginary doors for people? Just as we don't see actors acting out their jobs (I immediately take that back), we don't see woodworkers obscuring their screwing hands, for example, in a cunning attempt to hide their screwing shortcomings.

Nor do we see them looking as though they've seen a ghost when they forget what they've done with the screws, or their foreman mouthing to them, 'Keep screwing, you're doing great', or doorway owners showing their appreciation for their work by announcing, 'I just long to be close to you'. Because that would all be too unbelievable for *properly* voiced words.

Unspecial CGI Effects

Jaws' huge success in the seventies didn't put off the producers of the recent shark film, *The Meg,* who, in 2018, went back into the waters – durr-dum – but not with a bigger boat, as per Chief Brody's iconic* instructions, but with a bigger shark …made this time from saltwater proof but, quite evidently, not idiot proof CGI. *Dumb-durr*!

However, despite *The Meg's* poor ratings, its producers can be forgiven for giving over the main mischief-maker role in their film to computer graphics, for the regrettable reasons that we're so easily fooled by them, and that the golden age of Hollywood died out around the same time as the Megalodons.

———————

*And, in view of the circumstances, wise.

Second Serve Fault

Anyone for tennis?

Get your tickets 'ere, ladies and gents. Come and see the freaky giant men, known in the trade as servebots, play the Victorian game of tennis, and let them amaze you with their famous hammering down of tennis balls at 150mph before your very eyes.

Come on, come on, don't be scared – these monsters aren't that frightening, and they aren't machines, which is why we allow them the curiosity of having two goes at walloping the ball down, should they mess the first one up. Nowhere else will you be able to see such a spectacle, ladies and gents, particularly in the attraction of sport, where failure like this is rewarded with another go. The knife-throwing lady next door is, sadly, proof of that.

Anyone??

Tripe, Waffle And Crepe For Breakfast

When BBC's *Breakfast TV* first appeared in the UK in 1983, it was so radical and exciting that it caused a severe shortage of eggs, pigs, brown sauce and able-bodied employees.

Now, unfortunately, the Beeb's top-of-the-morning fixture of news and infotainment is toast, and has also rung in sick*. Long gone are its days of high calorific sofa delight, now replaced, it appears, with a soporific three hour set menu presentation of tripe, waffle and crepe, which even pigs, of whom, thankfully, there are now droves, would do well to avoid.

---

*Thank goodness, then, for the fabulously fattening Piers Morgan, currently on ITV.

Swords Drawn

Following the 2018 World Chess Championship, which, after 19 days of brutal non-committal competition, ended in 12 drawn games out of 12 – a list of new official chess moves has been introduced:

- ➢ Knight takes pawn …to the seaside for a nice day out
- ➢ Queen checks king …is doing alright after his recent fall
- ➢ Bishops smother king …with kisses and general messages of good will
- ➢ Pawn squeezes knight …on the cheek for taking him out
- ➢ Queen pins rook …down on the couch while the king is laid up upstairs
- ➢ King presses …his good ear and leg to the floor
- ➢ Rook forks queen …with tempo

Mate. *At last.*

Munchausen 1 Veracity ⊗

Yes team!

You can keep your Cruyff turn or Messi flick, what this club's got is the ability to perform convincingly on the big stage. A pretend feign, a quick swerve of the truth, some bawling out loud and a bit of dribbling from the corner of the ~~box~~ mouth – skills like these win football matches*.

You're one up. Now go out there again and don't lose your lead, i.e. the main protagonist, to a real retaliatory foul, which will really, really, *really* hurt.

––––––––––

*And film studio offers.

The Social Effete

Another day, another A-list celebrity rashly hacks off their social media arm. While such amputations are usually performed in a sterile way, rendering the now de-listed celeb free from living germs, they're often carried out in fits of pique, with little thought about the after-affects.

Subsequently, it's only when the patient is made aware of how the operation went that the real agony begins. In a few cases, the healing process is quick and the celebrity gets used to their new found lame. But often the lopping-off procedure lacks the necessary skills and precision needed to prevent going green from setting in, resulting in their sudden desperate wish to have their arm back – regardless of how ugly it was getting.

Perhaps they just need reminding that it's God's plan* to make all media arms precious!

_____

*As in marketing.

Clap Trap

Showing tonight at cinemas everywhere, a classic tale of good versus self-congratulatory idiocy.

Chief Brody, of Amity Island fame, shoots and finally kills a big toothy shark and some onlookers* start clapping in a spontaneous call to arms, but mainly hands, to show their relief and approval. Tellingly, though, the filmmaker, Mr Spielberg, didn't include scenes of Amity Gazette readers, or Local News viewers, celebrating this joyous news in the same manner, because that would've been a clappy ending to a great film – and people in real life** just don't do that.

---

*In the cinema.
**Outside the cinema.

Lesser Spotted Celebrity

People snapping up gossip mags of celebrities snapping their heels at the snapping paparazzi, and snapping them up even more (the mags) when they start snapping at them for snapping them.

With all this sneaky snapping going on, we'd have thought it would've been a snap for the whole fiasco to have completely snapped by now, but far from it. The symbiotic threesome is as stable as a pap's tripod, whose latest assignment, coincidentally, is to capture just that.

There's only one way to break out of this tedious, endless, loop …one of the legs must snap out of it. And if you're thinking what I'm thinking – then snap!

Just Unfairway

Golf.

The noble game of honour, equality and fair play. Unless, that is, we happen to be packing a few quid in our back pockets, behind the score-card, in which case we can just pull out our custom made precision driver, with adjustable perimeter weighting and heavy bias in our favour, and hoick for six* our unique, spherically-tiled, tetrahedral, catenary, aerody-namic ball – plus any remaining notion of glory, parity and fairness.

See you on the green.

---

*A cricketing term, usually referring to someone with fortune on their side, who's not playing with a straight bat**.
**Another cricketing term.

As Easy As One TV

In a very recent study (this one), it is postulated that at the centre of our universe lurks TV101 – a supermassive, blackest of blacks, black hole, which spans about 1.4 billion nanometres across diagonally (55 inches), and that is getting bigger and clearer each year.

The gravity of this abyss is so strong that it warps both our living space and, crucially, much of our waking time – a quarter of it, according to recent studies. Sadly, it seems that life itself, the smartest, but also, by definition, the stupidest thing in the known cosmos, is unable to escape its pull.

There's one thing we can do to save us, and that's to singularity wormhole ourselves away from the telly more often*, and to channel our energies to escape to new event horizons*, and to much more rewarding, and less remote*, lives.

———————

*Flannel hopping.

Squash No Let

Faster, Higher, Stronger.

Presumably, this famous Olympic motto is not a summary of the organisation's commercial dexterity*, but a nod to all those competing in the multi-sport Olympic Games. So for squash, which is commonly voted the healthiest and most physical sport (unless we happen to be stupendously wayward at golf), and boasts arguably the fastest, highest and strongest competitors of all, never to have been included *Khan* not be right.

The World Squash Federation should stop hitting their head against the walls and just *Nicol* the IOC's stockpiles of money instead – thus, driving them back to what the fundamentals of sport should be all about …and to the use of a tin.

---

*Despite, by chance, the three words perfectly summing up the spirit of the IOC's sweaty business of making so much cash so quickly, and then having to stash it away in secure vaults in tax-free Switzerland.

Sun Night Bloody Sun Night

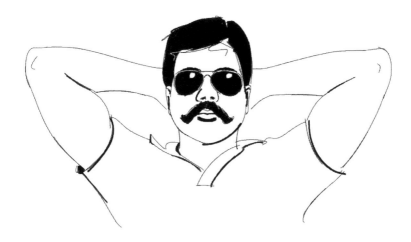

For countless celebrities, the dim* behaviour of wearing sunglasses in all weathers, but particularly indoors and at night, is merely a way of shielding themselves from the harmful effects of being in *The Sun* too much.

We may stigmatise such conduct as short-sighted at best**, as daylight is often hours away, but perhaps our brightest stars – like Bono – who have incurable sun shining out of their bottoms (in addition to a less than jocular ocular condition) are doing us all a great favour by wearing them …in the retinal-damaging event of starlight blowback.

---

*And shady.
**And pitifully megalomaniacal at worst.

Crowd Kneel To Football's Billions

Commentary on today's game comes from Gold Trafford.

Neat one-two there between TV money and bloated billionaire, before passing the cash to corporate club. Clubbo dribbles much of it away on greedy agents and overpaid players, but is soon on the ball again after requesting more subs from bloats. The crowd thinks it's all clover but, deep down in their pockets, they're angry with all the money hogging – klaxon, 'we're forever paying double' and klaxon-klaxon, 'who's the banker with the stack' ring out, as we go into the make or break.

The score remains at billions to kneel. We'll be back after these short, but stern, messages.

Stop being greedy with the ball (*you arsehole*)
Stop fouling fans (*you arsehole*)
Stop trying to dictate play (*you arsehole*)
Otherwise, you multiple arsehole, you're off!

You Cannot Be Furious

Weed control, smashed-racket style.
Crowd control, kung-fu-kick style.
No ball control, flung-clubs style.
Chest control, headbutt style.
Complete loss of control, bitey-ear style.

For purveyors of such crude and unsporting behaviour, of which there are hordes – and include many a talented and upstanding household name* – their PATHETIC (petulant annoyance and testy hostile enragement, with touchy ill-mannered cockiness) outbursts of aggressive frustration (OAF), often against inanimate objects, Basil-Fawlty style, are absolutely ~~not on~~ not to be missed.

---

*Which may, therefore, preclude the name Nick Kyrgios.

Charlie And The Recirculate Factory

If, in a lazy attempt to make a big splash in the art world, we were to trace over a Hockney with state-of-the-art paints and brushes then, arrogantly, try to palm it off as a more polished version of the original, we would rightly get a headfirst-lobbing into the nearest swimming pool, with several bricks attached to our legs.

It's unfortunate, then, that the same principles aren't reflected in the movie industry, where *Dumbo* filmmakers in their director's chairs are continually remaking earlier films with almost *Total Recall*, while *Texas Chainsaw Massacring* them in the process. The *Psycho* studio bosses should stop playing *Footloose* by treading crudely over old ground and going for easy targets*. Else, we'll reboot them into the nearest *Wicker Man* and set it ablaze.

…Or, better still, sit them in front of the remake**.

---

*Like *King Kong*.
**With several chainsaw massacring psychos attached to their legs.

All Set On Quiet, Nine Take

Ah, the magic of movies.

A time to put our feet up with a large barrel of popcorn and to suspend all disbelief for a few hours. But there is a limit. Not to the amount of popcorn, but to the amount of disbelief we're expected to suspend.

We're not talking about there being no way, for example, a shark can stay down with three barrels on him. No way! We're talking continuity errors, which, unfortunately, even great movies like *Jaws* fall victim to. Such as, for instance, the ever-changing number of barrels aboard Quint's boat in the final scenes, which, clearly and unbelievably, the script supervisor had trouble counting – presumably because they were too busy filling them up with popcorn …for added buoyancy …and bait.

Smile you son of a switch!

The Ref's Derision Is Final

If I was a postman who'd been "inadvertently" trampling across number 66's Wembley-like lawn, and over their prized, cup-winning, tulips in an effort to take the shortest path, then the least I should expect to pay is the penalty of a stern telling off, if not straight up, showy, yellow and red cards. Undoubtedly, it was my mistake, and mine alone, for not managing the situation better by taking the non-prize-winning, longer, path.

Now I could at this point, in the post-latch analysis, proceed to make an even bigger fool of myself by immediately going on national TV to take out my embarrassment and muddy, petal-littered, shoes on the owners – and to slag them off as disgraceful cheats who don't know what they're doing, and for making my job harder, and for causing me to drop two joints.

But that would be an absolute shocker of a decision by me. Not least because we all know how difficult a job managing gardens is.

Fee-Fi-Forced-Fun

I smell the fraud of everyone.

Call us boring old farts who love counting beans in attics, but not all of us are excitable exhibitionists, or alcoholics, who enjoy being thrust into settings of fake fun and forced frivolity. Parties, weddings, New Year, family get-togethers, funerals* and – the epitome of spurious merriment – work events. It's like one giant pantomime**, apart from the better rehearsed acting.

If we want to genuinely cultivate a good time then we should axe these convincing, but excruciatingly miserable, theatrics from our lives. We might just be amazed at the riches that sprout up as a result.

---

*It's what he would have wanted.
**Pinocchio.

I Name This Ship Sponsorship

With all the subtlety of a Dunkin' Donuts slam dunk aboard an American Express train, historic sporting venues are, preposterously, being constantly renamed in honour of their Target sponsors, who are paying an Arm & Hammer for the privilege. The King Power these companies wield is ridiculous. Frankly, it's an absolute Liberty.

I suppose, though, to be fair, the owners are stuck between a Hard Rock and a hard place. Do they stick to their Wankdorf heritage, or suck it up and rename their stadium Middlefart, for example? Of Coors, we can Bet365 our bottom dollar that, in the end, money will always Keepmoat owners sweet. Nevertheless, for Citizens like us, naming rights have gone Wells Fargo too far now, and Lord's only knows where it will all end.

Gymnauseam

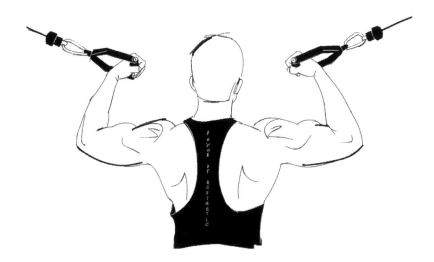

Mirror mirror on the wall, who's the sleaziest of them all?

Gym bunnies, that's who. While, for a select few of us, this place of worship might be the healthiest on Earth*, for the majority, it's the ghastliest and smelliest place, not to mention, very often, the spindliest**.

So welcome to the club. A frighteningly expensive hall of mirrors that reflects true, but unkindly, on man's obsessive and loathsome love of himself. Where the quads and glutes and delts and pects, are the gods of brutes and svelte and sex.

If only we could see ourselves.

---

*Outside of Holland and Barrett.
**Re the weedy, stick-like, legs, usually shown off by top-heavy gents, whose minds, ironically, are solely on down below.

The Definition Of Old

Having watched far too much TV in our time, as mentioned in the earlier episode 'As Easy As One TV' (page 47, catch it now on thigh player), it's fair to say our spacetime has been warped. Not just by the inherent abyssal gravity of TV, as stated, but also by the picture quality and, seemingly, lack thereof as we head back in time.

Think of the shocking images of 2001, for instance, or the murky ones of eighties sitcoms, such as *Mind Your Language*, or the downright filthy and disgusting ones of seventies *Steptoe and Son*. Weirdly, though, and taking technology into account, these programmes definitely seemed Sharp to us at the time, and nothing like the blurry pictures we see of them nowadays.

So what's happened?

Well, the answer is easy. TV, like time and space, is a great big illusion, and recordings of it, along with memories, are subject to grav…………... Sorry, we appear to have lost this evening's episode. While we try to fix the problem, here's an old episode of *The Good Old Days*.

The Chase Is Not Off

As daytime TV programmes go, ITV's *The Chase* is a million steps ahead of the chasing pack, so much so, in fact, that we could almost give it next year's television award now. But there's one thing standing in its way – the piss easy, repetitive and almost pointless* questions.

So let the piss easy, repetitive and almost pointless questions begin.

Which pop artist's name rhymes with handy snore hole?
Which American space agency Never Applauds Stupid Answers?
Which son of God probably had an itchy beard?
Which oh not so quiet Icelandic singer watched two episodes of a private fictional detective on TV last night, before retiring to bed in her house made of ice, whose name (the house's) rhymes with pigpoo?

Jesus. Unless we've been in a coma for the past ten years, or on a large rocky body that orbits our planet, then there's only ever one plausible answer to all these elementary questions. To just switch off.

---

*The close runner-up in the head-to-head …if not, by now, the clear leader of the pack.

Fⓧr The Recⓧrd

It's almost official. We are a record breaking bunch of show offs who are desperate to impress at all times, as long as it involves little to no skill or effort. All we need now is an audience with the Guinness World Records team – for a fee – to prove it*.

We can amazingly quickly skip over commendable records of the past, such as the world's fattest man, and bring forth today's cash cow of dubiously superlative, small-stomached, big heads …like the man who can drink 200ml of mustard in 13.9 seconds, or the (one assumes different) man with a collection of 6,290 sick bags, or the (still one assumes different) man who can unravel a whole toilet roll with one hand in 9.8 seconds, on a Tuesday.

Next up on stage, no doubt – furthest projectile vomiting.

---

*A process that, for an even further, heavier, fee**, can be fast-tracked so we can officially become a moron quicker than anyone else.

**No guesses, then, for who holds the record for, 'The fastest hands rubbed together'.

Stumped By Silly Point

Welcome to summer, and to today's game of cricket.

Listen carefully. That is the sound of the crowd briskly rubbing its hands together in anticipation of an exciting day's play, and to get some feeling back in their fingers. Sadly, they're about to be doubly disappointed.

So let loose the men in white coats, to pitch to the crowd their curious cricketing competence, and to remind us what summer's all about – picnics, strolling around the park and watching the least athletic people since wafting at flies and sandwich eating were both dropped from Olympic competition.

As predicted – heavy snoring stops play. Today's action-packed highlights then …man successfully fields 14th drink after 13 looseners, batsman releases pent-up energy by whacking out hard at googlies, female ducks, man woken up by bad dream that he's at the cricket, commentator hammers bails into eyes and cricket gets all defensive after being declared truly and utterly *out*!

Seating Pan

We've been looking forward to this for months – a night out at the theatre! And no expense spared, either, having found half-price tickets for the stalls.

Tonight's performance will start in two sentences. Please take your seats.

An eager peak towards our seats reveals nobody sitting in front of us. *Wicked*! We've just got time to see how many people are noticing how well-off we are*(n't)*, before a final bow by us and then …*Mamma Mia!* and *Jesus Christ super stare*! Edging down the row in front are the world's tallest, and tardiest, couple who, probably on a day off from playing giraffes in *The Lion King*, are about to completely spoil our view!

Oh well. Let's hope our forthcoming prods of contempt and audible quips about it snowing up there (re the bad dandruff) will make things a bit more bearable for us. If not then the less than giant leg room for them *certainly* will.

NL YCNN CTS HT*

Awkward, clever, anti-TV, currently on BBC2 (lifted from BBC floor).

The connection? …*Only Connect*. The puzzling TV game show with more than half the pieces missing from that which is typically shown on the box these days, but which still manages to come together perfectly. It just takes a bit of lateral thinking to work out, that's all.

No half-wits connect with no easy questions, that connect with no gimmicks, that connect with no televisual atmosphere, that connects with no chitchat, that connects with no hee-hee or ha-ha – all of which means a clear disconnect from the stupid, shiny and overly friendly ambience that's very much connected with the banality of today's mainstream TV.

Fantastic. We've finally figured something out.

---

*Answer: Only Connect is a hit (not shit).

The Bizarre Strangled Banner

America. As the world's biggest producer and consumer of pornography, we can rightly assume that Americans are no less inhibited on the subject of nudity and sex than the rest of us – unless they've all been watching it in dungeons with hoods on (as can be peeped at in the bonus scene in *Robin Do'es* Marian*).

So this begs the question, then, why they put up with their long-time partner like they do, i.e. the Federal Government, who has such a prudish aversion to the subject. Take no offence, but the human body, and parts thereof, should be no more censored, pixelated or blurred, for an adult TV-watching public, than accepting as the norm, from birth, the obscenely vulgar and perverted showing of erect guns everywhere.

Sham! Bang! Fuck you Sam.

---

*Dominates.

Game, Set And Scratch

Ace! The tennis is on, but we haven't netted ourselves a ticket, and we can't seem to lay a racket on a TV, either. Grunt! The penalty for these amateurish, unforced, errors is that we'll just have to listen to it on the radio instead. Balls.

Quiet please. Commentators. Ready. Play.

Cue a stunning volley of unimaginably difficult to read comments about crosscourt backhands from the deuce court, into left forehand corners of right baselines, retuned with forehand spin down some other line or two, before a mini break for breath and a continuing rally of indecipherable servings that pass way over our heads at all times, which means a sudden, but not before time, backspin dink to Classic FM.

New calls.

We Are Not Binge-Worthy

24 hours solid, fastened to the sofa like a health hazard label, with *The Good Wife* beside us. Unable to move our butts but for the odd *Peaky* through the *Blinders* to see where the takeaway is, and *The Walking Dead* ascent up *The Staircase* for the *Game of Thrones**. Why do these shows have to be so *Breaking Bad***?

One criticism. If the producers gave us time to scratch our arses between episodes – a traditional week's worth of scratching would be most gratifying – instead of dispensing them like cheap drugs, which they can't satisfy demand for, then the deferred viewing pleasure would make them even more enjoyable and leave us feeling less *Lost**** at the end. *Stranger Things* might happen!

Anyway, for now, your next chapter will begin in 5 seconds …or after the one and only (obvious) continuity error.

---

*Loo.

**Dope.

***Not on my watch.

@!*#?

Strangely deranged

Thesaurus
piety, fix, protection, vanity, toned, SOS, potty, chocolate, joy, delete, rotten, art, forgery, terminal, frightful, pants, leggy, wordy, imagine, fowl, childish, meow, territory, green, Doris, nirvana, unstable, Martin, cushion, oblivion

Evolution = Monkey Minus Church

No, this isn't a depiction of a London street scene, near the church, the one by the zoo, it's a portrayal of man's rise through millions of years of evolution – from lowly apes and sneaky apes with knives, to holy baloney creepy apes with phoney symbolic lives.

And, again, no, those aren't my harsh words, they're practically the smart, sharp and upright words of Albert Einstein, when he said that religion is a product of human weakness and primitive superstition, as celebrated in the aforementioned equation E = m-c.

Fr⊗m Asthm⊗ T⊗ An⊗them⊗

As a former chronic user of shady blue puff-puff*, I like to think I'm not a total smackhead when it comes to understanding the highs and lows of hard drugs – for example, bending over with one of those inhalers in your pocket doesn't half chafe your thigh.

But just the thought of shooting up even harder gear to get oneself through life's inevitable uphill struggles, which, coincidentally, puff-puff was specially designed to do, is enough to make me relapse into a little non-exercise-induced bronchoconstriction.

---

*AKA Salbutamol: *Wheezy to Eazy in just two puffs*. Always read the label.

For Our Health Ban Safety

CAUTION!!!!!!!!!!!!!!!!!!! The following story contains nuts, which some may find depressing.

Once upon a time, in Earth's greaterstoic era (pre eighties), we all lived carefree. It was a time where any signs of caution, of which there were few, were duly frisbeed to the wind – and it was an age where high viz was generated by moving around*, rather than just appearing extremely yellow.

Thinking back to that time, we'd absolutely choke at the thought of not using plastic parts, and the bags they came in, as toys. Or being advised by Ruislip Manor tube station to be careful as the recent wet weather may cause wetness. Or having to live, in general, in today's innately bananas and greatly*pathetic* era.

This *truly* dangerous obstacle needs reversing!

---

*Over more uneven and slippery surfaces the better.

Worrying Hair

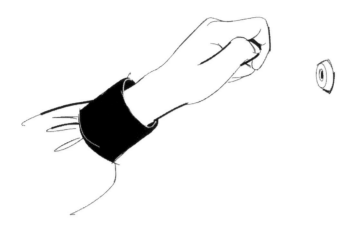

Knock-knock.

Who's there.

A stranger.

Hang on a second, please, while I have a sudden urge to flick my hair into place before opening up, even though there's less than zero chance of you knowing whether I've had a bad hair day or not, or if I've just generally let myself go recently.

Unless it's our hairdresser checking on their latest handiwork (a completely hairbrained idea) then those few seconds of primal worrying and faffing around are better spent just telling them to go away …and that we'll brush it properly later.

Bend And Stretch. Now The Other Finger.

Wearing fitness apps.

Who cares if people think we're on the run from the local intensive care unit, following a somewhat miraculous recovery, because these things help us to shed the pounds*, tune up** and look good!***.

_____

*£200 shed before we even set off, followed by 350 calories per stroll – mainly through checking our emails at every hint of a stitch, chatting to Nancy and Barb on a three-way, taking photos of fresh dog trumps on less fresh tree stumps, and flaunting our wears to other passing outpatients.
**U2's 'Running to Stand Still' on repeat.
***Eight likes per amble is not unheard of, which doesn't include Nancy and Barb.

Alarm Bell Death Knell

There's only one thing more disturbing than being woken by our house alarms – and that's when they're attached to somebody else's house. This is because:

a) they're louder than the Big Bang, and continue for about as long; and
b) they're usually set off by nothing more sinister than a passing elderly couple in matching balaclavas and hearing aids (doubtless deafened by decades of alarm abuse) or by less coordinated fallen leaves.

The loud sounds might save the noisy neighbours a few pounds on insurance, and scare the odd fox, but, paradoxically, their noise (the alarms') is enough to make any upstanding, sleep-deprived, person want to go out and ransack the place …which, obviously, explains the old couple's heading.

30p A Plop

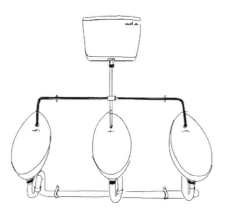

It absolutely *stinks* to have to pay to use public toilets, whether it's for just a quick tinkle or for a more drawn-out doo-doo. Either way, it's a shockingly foul business that makes millions from our blameless bladders, and where the only barriers to entry, it seems, are a couple of murky turn stiles, presumably soiled – for free – by non-coin collectors and fantastically ironic dogs.

Next time we'll remember to bring a bottle.

And cork.

Sub-Quality Of Old

Chocolate is chocolate. However, all is not quite so doubly sweet with Nestlé's Quality Street. As a taster:

- Strawberry Delight, *is far from right* – sicklier than a Christmas get together, or holiday gathering of any sort
- Toffee Penny, *left with many* – good only for leveraging confectionary tubs open with and for plugging holes in chocolate manufacturer's profit sheets (and boats)
- Orange Crème, *a dentist's dream* – (see Strawberry Delight)
- The Purple One, *the prince of peeves* – too confident, too runny, two in the ~~tin~~ tub if we're lucky

All encased in said smooth, round, magically-shrinking* ~~tin~~ tub, with just enough chocolates to conceal the base.

Re-treat!

---

*Which we all know the trick to.

Not Funny Ha Ha

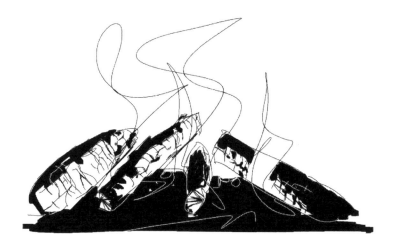

Be it a colleague telling us about their aunt's sudden face-first fall into a burning fireplace, or a knock on the door for a lost, three-legged, blind puppy, we can take much satisfaction in knowing that both sets of "worrying" events are likely to have a happy ending …for us at least.

Because, while schadenfreude may not be the easiest of emotions to admit having or – with missing dentures and a fat lip – to say, it's certainly one we all truly, and *properly* worryingly, share.

Thank god aunt Maudie wasn't instantly cremated, otherwise our secret, grubby, delight might not have been containable.

The Cat's Tongue Tale

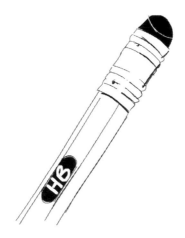

We've made an error in our economics exam – money doesn't, in fact, grow on trees anymore. But fear not, we've atop our definitely tree-grown pencil, a small, pert, tongue-coloured eraser, which, if it was also of tree heritage, would easily rectify our mistake. But, regrettably, it isn't and, so, it doesn't.

Instead, manufacturers seem to prefer making it out of a combo of actual cat tongue (called Smudge, prior to its stuffing) and equally gone-off Hubba Bubba – both of which are notorious for making a right mess of our faces if we're not careful.

Say Eeurrghh

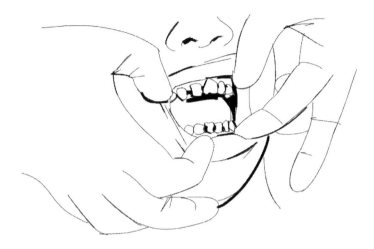

With dazzling role models like Clarkson, Fry and Bowie (pre *Black Tie White Teeth* album), it's Little Wonder that us Brits are so comfortable with, and rooted in, having natural* looking teeth. But if only our pride and identity extended to dentistry then we wouldn't have to be so tight lipped about what is, unfortunately, our national theme:

God save our monstrous teeth
Long live our woeful teeth
God save our teeth
Send them victorious
Snappy and glamorous
Long to remain with us
God save our teeth

———————

*Code for wonky, gappy, chipped, stained and rotten. OMG, nurse, nurse!!

Arthritic Art

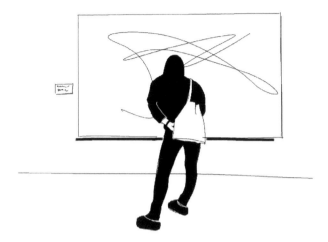

Artritis: rhymes with detritus; a term used to describe the current condition of the arts.

Symptoms: a painful stiffness that causes significant swelling of the ego and subsequent immobility of all creativity. For example, music sampling, book/movie sequels and remakes, saggy ass jeans, turds on canvas – you get the picture …although hopefully not in that last example.

Causes: 90% general tear and wear of old ideas, which debilitates artistry and originality, 8% stock shock tactics and 1% laziness.

Treatment: a saggy turd in the face should help to elicit a much fresher response, after which a few more follow-ups *is*, in this instance, highly recommended.

Non To Fiction

Breathing. Eating. Lying.

Some of our most natural and vital bodily functions, if not the main three*. Remove just one of these woven strands of our very fabric and where would we be?

In all truth, though, perhaps we could survive without one of them – namely our constant embroidery of said truth, and start to weave our way down life's long and frequently slippery catwalk with a lot more class, respect and decorum. Naturally, however, after you.

By the way, I *hate* the dress.

---

*For fashion models, mincing outmanoeuvres eating.

Dirty Thousand Feet

 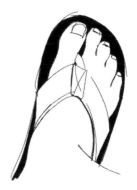

Now arriving.

A repugnant parade of cheesy toenail fungus, gout and general big toe insolence, interspersed with a flap-flap-flapping of moist, yet still flaky, athlete's foot upon rancid rubber.

Yes, for lots of us, close calls in airports with flip-flop wearers are turbulent experiences that often lead to bouts of ill will and emotion sickness. Great care, therefore, should be taken to avoid them. In the event of a sudden encounter with claw toes, we should adopt the grace position …and pray to God the cheese balls are flattened by the next available (heavily loaded) luggage truck.

Homework Doesn't

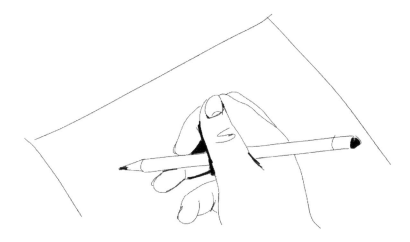

All homework and no play takes *The Shining* off Jack and Jill, making them dull and a little bit stir crazy. So, children, from now on, let's just overlook it and go and have a ball instead.

For kids: There'll be less stressing about impressing or progressing, and more being frugal with assessing, and Google. Excellent stuff.

For teachers: The axe will fall on all that terrifying, and murderous, red writing and marking. Textbook job, well done.

For parents: There'll be fewer family subtractions and divisions, resulting in positive outcomes for everyone. Nicely worked out.

For society: A-maze-ing understanding and progress will be made by all. Keep up the good (non-home) work.

Genital Thwarts

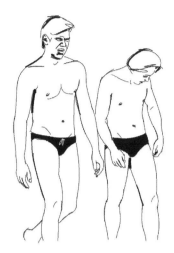

Men.

Tight-fitting, butt-hugging, ball-balancing, knob-revealing swim briefs. Fair dos, if we're an Olympic-level wrestler, diver or swimmer on medal day – then all power to our newly streamlined loins.

But while the sport of prancing around on sand and looking like a right nonce might, one day, be formally embraced by the Olympics*, for now, outside of these shockingly small windows of opportunity, there can be almost nowhere left to hide for such uncomfortable looking dicks.

_____

*Dressage makes it in, so who knows.

Crawl World

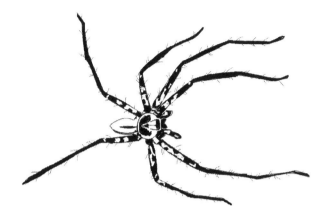

Most spiders have the vision of a bat and the weapons of a goldfish. So why, then, do we find these eight-eyed, alien-looking, creatures, which scurry around our feet with the speed, predictability and stopping power of a blown up, untied and released balloon, so scary?

Even the word spider – which used to be spelt spiiider until two legs got lopped off in a frenzied shoe attack – gives us the creeps. Experts believe this, seemingly, irrational fear is both evolutionary and hereditary, and more common in Europe, where spiders once carried deadly diseases that caused people to dance uncontrollably* …and where, also, one assumes, there are fewer shoes.

Tip: Having crawled the web**, it's noted that we can reduce our fear by exposing ourselves to brief alternating images of flowers and spiders, which effects our subconscious. Bonus tip: most spiders don't react well to having thick David Attenborough autobiographies dropped on them from heights …apart from, of course, the bionic-eyed jumping ones.

---

*They still have this effect on the wife.
**Genius.

Wordsmirch

Check out the synopsis of my new book, '*Repugnant Words*'…

Basically, Gordon Globule and Colin Cluster were best of wrestling rivals. Gordon was a rambunctious hunk, who could often be seen thrusting his super-lubed bulbous bosoms, without compunction, while tucking into a side salad and a bountiful amuse-bouche of moist ganache, with dollops of coulis, also on the side.

Colin wasn't quite as refined, or as sticky. More the crusty, jaunty and plump sort, who preferred a medley of all the trimmings and gubbins, plus punnets of fruity roughage with crema – all of which helped to clear out his passages and crevices, but played havoc with his pustule-ridden, cruddy, mounds.

Clenched buttocks on stools everyone. A frisson of boisterous and juicy excitement abounds, as one of these two chumps is in for a right old ruddy smashing. Let's get ready to fumble! …and just hope their stagnant lycra panties contain any stray pubes.

Sounds almost too awful for words.

We're Forever Blowing Bubbles

Bed time.

Time for our asleep brains to dip its dipper in again and to blow one of those magical, colourful and short-lived bubbles over to our, subsequent, awake brains. As always, there's emotionally-charged writing on it but, as ever, our awake brain's butterfingers and doziness fails to grasp the significance of its message. Another universal Hollywood script lost to the ether.

Never mind. We won't let it stop us dreaming …of a time, say, when science's most roused of awake brains, wakes up even further to comprehend the gravity of our nightly black holes, and the incomprehensible amount of time* we each spend trapped in them.

---

*Six years or so.

Spikeful Birdbrains

Plop! There goes another one.
Splat! And another.
Shit! Is there no end to this turd!?

That's the vulgar and dirty business of putting up bird spikes in urban environments, aimed at deterring – if not skewering – fluffy, cute and singy birds from cohabiting with us. What great tits we are for allowing such fowl poop on our streets, and for robin birds of their freedom with our pigeon-hearted arrogance.

Pests like us, who display such intolerance to nature, need reminding of how lucky we are to coexist with these creatures at all, having previously soiled every nook and cranny of the planet – and then dropping from a height onto some horribly pointy railings … faeces first.

Still Going On 21

At the age of 51 and a half, going on 52, my body is starting to feel its age – with the notable exceptions of my state of mind and my nipples, which have never knowingly been used (the nipples) or tweaked (also just the nipples, as far as I know). So while my knees and most other bits and pieces are now aching to be 21 again, my mind really isn't, because that's how old it still feels. Which feels very, *very* odd.

Perhaps the relative retention of our shiny marbles in old age, compared to the lost cause of our bodies, comes down to our terrible immaturity as a species. Which reminds me. I have a big game of biggies this evening against dead-eye (and big) Trevor down at the Dell. Note to self – must remember knee pads and glasses, and to drop marbles along the way ………in order to get back home.

Nemesis 1

So God made all the animals – wild ones, tame ones, riled ones, lame ones. God saw that this was good. His road to creation included cats and their eyes, which he saw coming from a long way off. But it's too late now, a new God's in town – and about to undo all the good work.

Day 1: Let there be light, so we can tally up how many animals succumbed to our villainy last night*.

Day 2: Let there be sky, for the purpose of letting there be birds.

Day 3: Let there be earth and vegetation, so we can ambush anything that moves, including stray bags, dogs and children.

Day 4: Let there be sun, moon and stars, so we can look up and laugh out loud.

Day 5: Let there be birds, for the purpose of letting there be cats.

Day 6: Let there be humans, so we can give them breathing problems, the attitude of Satan and the eyes when they're on the loo.

Day 7: Let there be rest. And paws.

Cute.

---

*50 million, give or take.

Spaced Out

Space: the final frontier.

These are the voyages of the Starship Monopolise. Its continuing mission: to explore strange worlds of personal seating space, to seek out new lowlife and uncivilisations, to boldly embargo where no one has done before.

Such as bursting our protective bubble when we take up an entire park bench, with our arms spread-eagled across its length like an eagle, or, worse still, when we're asleep on it, not like an eagle. And such as slowly, but surely, nudging our forearms back into our designated half of the plane's armrest, where they've paid no more to belong. And such as slinging, discus-like, any of our bags, hats and coats that are occupying precious empty train seats.

We need to remember that self-serving bubbles like these, including those of universes, exist only to be buffeted and popped – regardless that there's *bound* to be another seat, and universe, available at any minute.

God's Buttocks And Brussels Sprouts

Long, long ago, and far away, there lived a people who didn't have the Time (mag) or Google that we've had to properly understand things, and so, naively, they had to make things up. Stuff like thunder being caused by God's buttocks, and evil spirits lurking in Brussels sprouts, hence the need for the cross sign …marked on the sprouts, not God's buttocks*.

But now, of course, we know better. Or, we should do. Yet, we know Edison didn't invent the (sprout-shaped) light bulb, but he still gets all the limelight. We know the Great Wall of China isn't visible from space**, yet it continues to get all the alien visitors. And we know that eating sprouts that have been on a dirty floor for five plus seconds is definitely, definitely, not going to kill us …provided, naturally, we remembered to cross them first.

---

*Although they may *also* exhibit such a sign, for all we still know.

**Nor, by the way, are God's buttocks, despite what some believers of the "Butterfly" Nebula think.

Doris Have Had Their Day

Congratulations, it's a boy/girl!

Next job, let's think of a name for it. Preferably one that will give the little littlun a free leg up in life, and make us feel ten feet tall in the process. Not Hoist, Stiletto or Ladder, which are hugely demented and unsafe, but one that's fleetingly fashionable and fun – like us. After much covetous consideration, and parental license, we've narrowed it down to three choices:

1. Rise up from the riff-raff, like a celebrity, and call our precious bundle of light Crystal Shanda, which goes sparklingly well with our surname Lear; or
2. Hedge our bets with a nice-sounding, double-barrelled poop-poop of two-bit mumbo-jumbo; or
3. Play it safe with plain Vanity.

Hoist it is then.

Surname? Byonesownpetard.

The Imperfect Getaway

If you received my earlier postcard OK (page 81) then you'll have seen how stressful going on holiday can be. Sadly, the promise of perfection in paradise is, most often, painfully presumptuous too.

For starters, we need a pee. But the water's too clear, and the couple with eyes on our knapsacks are bound to notice. Also holding back have been the hotel re last night's entertainment, which was nowhere up there with Cocker and Warnes where the brochure said it belongs. Plus, our room had a c view*, we had our wallet stolen, there was too much complimentary seaweed, the starfish looked fake, the sun came up too early, the toaster too late, the wi-fi was fi-wi**, there were too many Brits and the sunsets and burgers weren't as rare as the ones we get back home.

Quite honestly, we can't wait to return. To *true* perfection.

---

*As in crap.
**Ficking widiculous.

Survival Of The Skittish

How to survive the day?

I know, we'll climb a ladder in an empty cornfield to check if the earth is flat or not, taking care not to make the foolish mistake of walking under it (the ladder). Then, when atop the ladder, we'll also, curiously and faithfully, start wondering what life after death will be like, once the aliens in those distant UFOs have had their wicked way with us.

Not much else to report from up here, really. Just a few crop ovals, which, 100%, are circles from above; itchy palms; Bob, the ghost-like figure from number 17, scaring flying saucer-shaped birds with talk of dragons; a strange sense that we've experienced all this before; and a natural disposition to assume that anything weird or unknown has got to be real, just in case – like the scary horizon, which we can clearly see dropping off before us – it is.

We made it.

Box Not Clever

All hail the efficiency of 21st century internet shopping. A few simple clicks and our orders are virtually on our doors, like magic – having, typically, travelled all the way from China, unless we're buying a pair of homemade Dr. Martens, for example, or a single Aston Martin.

Regrettably, though, it's *at* our doors where the efficiency comes to a carbon-ceramic brake grinding halt. 5,000 miles of posthaste transportation, thwarted in the final two inches by us not being at home or by our 19th century, hapless-holed, letter boxes – through which, if the postie's lucky, strong and pushes hard enough, the stamp can just about get through.

Thus, assuming our parcel wasn't then skilfully lobbed over the gate, or even worse, awkwardly fobbed off with the neighbour, it means yet another one of those unnecessary backward treks to the sorting office …and more wear on our ~~soles~~* souls.

---

*~~Dr. Mertans'~~.

Parental Misguidance

Raising a firstborn. A responsibility fraught with danger, and which should only be undertaken if we're sure we can handle it.

First up, please surround ourselves with as many soft toys as possible, in case we lose our grip and the little angel face falls and breaks ~~an eyelash~~ a wing*. Also, ensure there's an excess of friends and family, too, to witness the stunt, otherwise, we can just post liberally on social media to gain that extra, hard-sought, recognition. Finally, as we know, lifting littluns up to the sky without first embalming them in sun cream, from head to bow, is likely to cause us to projectile vomit all over them – so don't forget those extra wipes.

Other than that, we look forward to doing absolutely *none* of the above with any subsequent offspring, who'll just have to be raised more naturally.

---

*Note: Having the Turbo 2020 pushchair on standby will get us to the hospital in time …for whichever one of us needs it most.

Game Over

Life! What a fun, multiplayer, open world, action, educational, role-playing, simulation*, temporary, adventure game that was. How are we going to beat *that*!?

Introducing its natural and quite honourable sequel – death! The problematic, single player, closed world, permanent*, puzzle game, which, while it obviously doesn't have the gameplay of life, offers, say those who've briefly demoed it, infinitely greater resolution* and liberation*. Plus a welcome guarantee.

Experienced gamers should be aware that achievements in life are not carried through to death, and that, unlike life, death does not come with basics, such as a controller, a field of view, power ups, extra lives, or a god mode* – all of which, of course, are sold (to death*) separately.

---

*Controversial.

LIFESTYLE

Smug is the drug

Thesaurus

bang, cock, mongrel, barrier, reward, awake, walkies, fatuous, indulge,
synthetic, carnivore, shelve, woolly, fawn, tick, befuddled, education,
washed, brainwashed, escapade, lardaceous, preen, coddle, plop, joyride,
threshold, tardy

Shoot 'Em Up

According to logic and American history, and also the patent application, guns were invented to kill. Shoot forward a millennia and the patent is now rif(l)e with an arsenal* of amendments, like the all-important second one, which reads, 'Guns are so wonderful and versatile that they can be used to attack and defend at the same time.'

Today, however, in almost the laughable words of Captain Mainwaring, we now have the most invaluable weapon in our fight for greater gun control – that of *non*-American history and logic**, which should, eventually, point us in the right direction …skywards.

---

*Three puns too many.
**Frazier: 'That's two.'

We Have A New Message

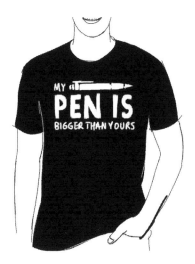

Message deleted.

Sure, when we eagerly parade such merriment on our chests we might think we're projecting ourselves as swanky and amusing, plus exceptionally gifted lovers. But unless we can back up our pithy proclamations with duplicate messages *beneath* the cloth, i.e. in actual ink format*, then our memos of mirth are as empty and impotent as the above gentleman's pen.

N.B. Tats get on my tits too (which only complicates matters).

---

*By way of more committed tats**.
**Tattoos.

Dog Turds

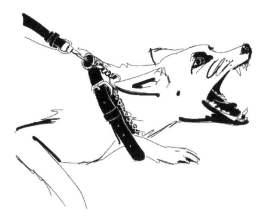

Immature man, 17-25, with chip on shoulder seeks young, fit and aggressive-looking dog* for submissive role-playing games and occasional walks around the block to get fags**, possibly more. Looks very important, so no time wasting poodles or sausage dogs. Must enjoy canned food, chains and being tied up.

Not well-endowed in any department so keen to act this fantasy out. Into most things as long as it provokes pain and misery, and, *obviously*, makes me feel well hard.

---

*Of the canine kind, with or without shoulder chip.
**Mainly of the cigarette kind.

Robin Rich Cedar Breast

It's that time of decade again when the needy garden fence begins losing its artificial colour*, and so, because brushing requires hammock disembarkment and some effort, we'll pull out our .44 spray gun o'nine shades, along with cedar-coloured bullets this time, and extra-long nozzle.

But, unfortunately, while the red misted firearm certainly stains the fence in a shot, excluding crevasses, collateral contamination can cause complications. For example, it's likely that such everyday staining sorties are not only the real root cause of so-called Saharan dust and fake tans but also of the bright breastages of robins. Cheep-cheep.

---

*Keeping-up-with-the-Joneses Jade.

The Risk Of Not Taking Any

To be skateboarding in front of a sunset, or not to be skateboarding in front of a sunset. Instead, just sitting down quietly and taking it in from what looks like the comfort of a harmless old bench but which, in truth, isn't, especially when the sun's going to take at least another 30 minutes before it sets to its most profound position, and we're not sure if our backsides are going to be able to take much more of this. That is the question.

'tis definitely nobler of the mind to suffer the scrapes and dull aches of a life well skated than to be sitting idly on our bums, only to suffer the same inevitable results.

40 Thinks

Unless our sex life's gone off the boil, or we have a gas hob, then the last place we should be thinking too much is in bed. But try telling that to our deranged brains when we're too often struggling to simmer down to a good night's sleep.

Annoyingly, just two minutes ago downstairs, we were managing to suspend consciousness like babies to the very loud sound of Metallica's 'Enter Sandman' – in concert with the neighbour's even louder banging – and now, when we actually want to properly exit light for never-never land, our minds just won't let us.

Now I lay me down to sleep
I pray the Lord to rule out sheep

Dumbilical Cords

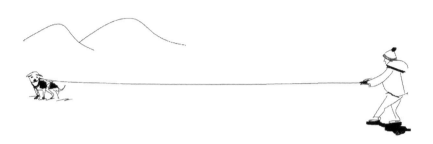

A wagging rear end, some eager panting and a bit of drool. Sadly, it's no adult dream, it's time to take Brian* for a walk. Cue a blow of the cheeks (by us) and the extra-long lead – not to power up the doggy treadmill again, but for us to accompany him this time, or to within a few hundred metres, or so, on his travels.

Sure, we could just dangle the lead through the letter box and let nature take its course, as it comes with a disturbingly powerful retraction mechanism (the lead), but if we did that we'd be missing out on an entertaining half hour in the life of Brian, and his spurious freedom, unwittingly tripping up ramblers en masse and tying himself up in very, very, very humorous knots.

---

*The dog.

Murder, Well Done, And Large Thighs, Please

Our fundamental craving for murderously fatty foods goes way back to our cave days, where such tasty goodness was so scarce that it was strictly only consumed on blowout Fridays. Plus at Christmas.

Fast forward fousands* of flabby Fridays later and, strangely, our evolutionary-led appetite for such foods has barely changed, despite its now overabundance and mischievous mocking of our mortality. The only positive in this fatuous modern world of fast food – and good takeaway – is that it gives us no end of time to work on our thighs.

I'm shovin' it.

_____

*Because fifty five is nowhere near enough.

Great Pandering Sanctuary

With hordes of us parents out there with ketchup, musical toothbrushes and iPads on continual stand, and sit, by, we might be forgiven for thinking the art of parenting these days has become nothing more difficult than child's play …such as hot potato.

If not then how else do we explain why we're always trying tomato everything fun and rewarding for kids, regardless of how important it is for *them* that they do the job – like ice creaming out the bedroom cupboards, or putting a new coke of paint on the wall, or unloading the weekly truck load of sweets, crisps and fizzy drinks.

Son, have you seen our marbles?

Can't Be Grassed

Besides constantly having to be on their toes when counting their fingers, one might assume a postman's biggest headache would be dealing with us at our absolute worst in the mornings.

However, in a survey*, the ugliest thing they said they had to deal with wasn't number 17 without their wig on, or 38's hairy upper-inner thighs. It was plastic artificial lawns. Unsurprising, when we think about it, as these weed and realism-free garden toupees, with their striking sterility and homogeneous shade of toxic green, blend in to their natural sur-roundings about as seamlessly as newly missing wigs/thumbs.

---

*Of one.

We Are What We Meat

It might not sound appetising, especially to new-age vegans*, but man's exploitation of animals over recent aeons has served us all extremely well. We could say that, up until now, the meat's been *well done*.

Because if it wasn't for the likes of Stew Insteak back in the day, doing the daily protein and calcium run in his leather shoes and matching whip, then the planet would've long been overrun by now with people with leeks for spines and cauliflowers, the size of walnuts, for brains …plus, not forgetting, lots and lots of sheep and chickens, and many, many, many other delicious animals too.

---

*Virtually Empty Green Attentio-N Seekers. Visibly *Emaciated* Green Attentio-N Seekers would've been taking things too far.

Brain Stops Play

Given the gravity of Newton's first law of motion, which states that an object will remain at rest unless acted upon by an external force, is it any wonder there are more figurines and pictures of people looking extraordinarily busy in the world than there are affixed shelves to put them on?

If only the art of not shelving things and avoiding procrastination was taught at homes and in schools from a very young age. Just think about the possibilities.

Just *think* about it.

Hair Today, Long Tomorrow

For millennia, humans have been shedding unwanted body hair, mainly to escape insects and exorbitant hairdresser fees. Worryingly, though, as recent trends suggest, the hair-crazy parasites are back.

Januhairy: a chance for women to put aside their shavers, and partners.
Februwavy: wave goodbye to straight hair, and to this week's wages.
Marchhare: hair coiffured into two, floppy, ear-shaped buns.
Ape-real: toupee or not toupee.
Mane: the king of the jungle/lord of the flies.
Junedrop: shampoo and human interaction-free for 30 days.
Judye: somewhere over the rainbow.
Augmentust: wear hair right down to about there.
Septemperm: poodle back to the eighties.
Octobald: to baldly go where no mane has gone before.
Movember: make cash, grow a ~~tash~~ rash.
Decembeard: a month-long fix of beards and nits.

Time for a shave. And shower.

Thick Skinned

We'd have to be mad, English and enjoy going out in the midday sun to waste 75p a minute on sunbeds, of the indoor tanning kind, when, for precisely 75p a minute less, we can get naturally frazzled skin from the equally vicious circle of the above-mentioned sun.

Agreed, having a suntan in all weathers might make us feel good, and slowly but surely camouflage our other, marginally less dangerous, addiction for Nutella, but arms up those of us who also want to look leathery, wrinkly and cancery before our time?

And now the other arm.

Rushing Abound

Turkish proverb states, 'The devil takes a hand in what is done in haste.'
Irish proverb states, 'God made time, but man made haste.'
Finnish proverb states, 'Hurry, and you'll only get shithead kids.'

All profoundly wise and leisurely words indeed but, by way of contrast, let's take a look at today's other contestants…

Newish proverb states, 'Can't this internet go any quicker?'
Selfish proverb states, 'Can't this person go any quicker?'
Boyish proverb states, 'Can't this car go any quicker?'
Slavish proverb states, 'Can't this day go any quicker?'
Foolish proverb states, 'Can't this smell of roses go any quicker?'

And the winner …coming steadily, yet quickly, on the outside, …and, surely, to absolutely nobody's surprise …is time itself! …The thieving *can't*.

Licence To Alcohol

In today's taster session, let's try the subtly complex and fruity Serving of Plonk, modern day varietal.

We're getting alcohol. We're getting *consumed*.
We're getting away from here. We're getting *stuck in a rut here*.
We're getting dopamine. We're getting *dopy*.
We're getting relaxed. We're getting *agitated*.
We're getting rewarded. We're getting *punished*.
We're getting animated. We're getting *slow*.
We're getting liberated. We're getting *withdrawn*.
We're getting high. We're getting *low*.
We're getting intoxicated. We're getting *toxic*.
We're getting rosy-cheeked. We're getting *white as a sheet*.
We're getting used to this. Hopefully, we're *not* getting used to this.

We're getting away from here.

Flame's Soon Gone Out On Quadratic Permanganate

Latin, Greek myth, *real* numbers, Pythagoras, triangles (of the "ting" kind), Henry VIII, i before e, RE, poetry, hanging valleys, the periodic table and running around with a bean bag balanced on our heads.

Apart from the last one, listed above, which comes in surprisingly useful on pub quiz nights (re the skilful balancing of multiple drinks), hands up all those adults who've found that learning these things at school has been an absolute godsend.

Networking, where to get the cheapest alcohol, healthy living, manners, house buying, personal finance, renewable energy, mental health, DIY, first aid, Chinese, YouTubing, stardom/bus driving, and the dangers of stardom and of getting hold of cheap alcohol.

Now, hands up if you *can't* work out what the next question is.

Born Wrinkled And Stained

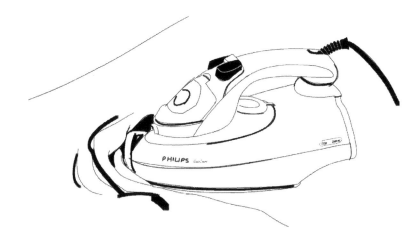

Provided we're not naturists, who enjoy showing off our wrinkles, then for nine and a half months of our lives, we find ourselves cooped up inside, and stooped over, in the fatal position of thinking that all of our laundry needs regular washing and ironing*. You name it, we'll cleanse and flatten it. Watch the powerful bursts of steam emerge from our ears, though, at just the thought of having to do it.

Agreed. If we're a sewage worker, wrestler or long-distance cyclist, who are continually getting our wares in a whiff, and twist, then *yes*, a regular spin through the two-fold wash-iron cycle, clearly, wouldn't go amiss. But, apart from the likes of these stenchful examples, consider the wash basket to be largely an empty case.

---

*Unless, again, we're men, who, for no other reason than that, leave it all to women anyway, in which case we *obviously* need a good hanging out to dry, and flattening with an incredibly hot iron.

I'm Just Popping Out, Mum

Why join our gang?

We're not like other gangs. We don't lure you into a contract killing straight away, or use scare tactics too frivolously:

Membership, Tools and Training
Lessons in how to walk, talk, make hand signals and commit acts of violence upon instruction. Also included is shanking for beginners, drill music* and a second-hand, slightly reddish, hoodie.

Support
New members receive a thorough beat in upon joining. Don't worry, our trained professional staff will keep you upright at all times during your journey of being bashed up, no matter how much of a bashing you get bashed up with.

Convenience
24/7 access to more than a thousand not-got-a-mind-of-their-own, like-minded, simpletons in this turf alone.

Community

Become a gang banger and you'll be joining a dope community of equally bored, thirst monster, prison-bound, deadbeats who, while we may lack all self-worth, respect and, any minute now, brain matter, are here to give you a nudge in the right direction. Luv bro.

_____

*Played at variable speeds and with hammer action.

Travel Sickness

Competition time. Where shall we ~~go to on holiday~~ adventure to this year?

Our friends, family and social media posse appear to be more grounded than we are and so, for sure, they'll be impressed by somewhere that's exotic and off the beaten track – a place where few superior show offs have been to, not even us. Furthermore, like Columbus and Amundsen beforehand, the journey to get there must seem risky and uncomfortable. It's at this juncture that we'll need to keep quiet, therefore, about any Club Class such travel, which, as anyone who's experienced it will appreciate, is much easier said than done.

…And then there are those who *really* think, in fact, that the world should be our adventure *down*-playground*, and that travel shouldn't be regarded as a sport or a game of scratch maps. But, all the same, as much as we respect their (narrow) view of the world, we couldn't disagree more, because – in the worldly, and quite hilarious, words of Columbus as he nav'd the med – that's Balearics!

----

*Such as our friends, family and social media posse.

The Rocket Science Diet

Want to reduce the size of our bulkheads? Then we should immediately abort the deployment of our current diet and exercise missions – which are a drag, and always affect our attitude and then stall – and transition to inject more aerodynamic fuel into our tanks*.

The supersonic component of this fuel is *good fat* – unlike the bad fat of, say, a Boost chocolate bar, whose consumption, albeit provides a quick, solid, burn that propels us off the launch pad, typically, results in the sudden and catastrophic explosion of fat everywhere.

The thrust of the argument is that intake of tasty good stuff for tasty bad stuff not only has enormous health benefits, including sleeker fuselages and stronger engines, but also affords us much lengthier flight paths and fuller tanks, for longer. The telemetry of our scales would appear to back up this new light plan.

---

*Such as ballast-busting blueberries and broccoli, payload-trimming whole-grain, centre of gravity-moving oily fish and legumes (nor me), and lift-off nuts, dairy, olive oil and oats. All washed down with plenty of ~~vodka wine beer coke diet coke~~ water.

Pride And Groom

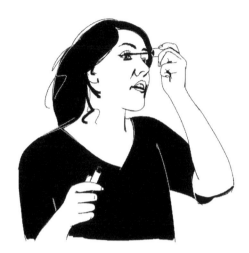

You join us here at the inaugural Checks Factor – a new talent show for pinheaded nitwits who relish grooming themselves in public.

First up on stage is plucky 22-year old Scarlett with, what can charitably be described as, a right medley of muck.

It's straight out with the mirror, then on with the light-sabre red lipstick and dusting of rouge. Already, there's unavoidable blush from some onlookers. Next, it's a quick pluck of the brows, and of stray nose hairs, before blowing out anything else that's underground up there on a tissue. A shrewd peak into the two-ply, followed by an equally wise two-way folding of it, indicates that there was. On with the show. A sudden leg lift is the signal for imminent flying toenail clippings, and to cover all cups, and then it's straight into the teeth picking – not by the crowd for bits of toenail, but by Scarlett for bits of gunge and red. Finally, there's a powerful burst of blackheads, and some equally strong sprays of Lynx and Dior.

Judges?

School Trip

In India, kids get to school by trekking across Himalayan glaciers. In Indonesia, they do so by walking across tightropes over raging rivers. In Britain, spooked by the abominably small chance that our loved ones might plummet down a moist, four-inch curb, and into the path of a car ambling along at 1mph*, we opt for the even more wobbly-kneed, chauffeur-driven, route.

Who cares that the inappropriately-named school run involves no sign of healthy running, unless we include the sprint to the heated front seats, or that it causes major air pollution, traffic problems and stress, and let's just make sure we get our kids from A to B in one piece, *OK* ...that's 'A' as in active and 'B' as in burdensome brats with breathing bother.

---

*Or yak speed, which, in the mornings and afternoons during school time, is a common sight on all UK roads.

Dog's Dollops

They say you can tell much about a nation by the way it treats its citizens when it's walking its dogs. Which means that Brits, like nearly all other packs of people, are, deep down, extremely friendly and approachable.

Forget any customary standoffishness, and bring to heel two complete strangers (in this setting, we don't know ourselves either) so we may create a bond of instant friendship through the social lubricant of our dogs, and perhaps, next time, partake in a park barbecue or campfire sing-song. And let's not worry about our usual chronic apathy for anything local, and promptly take on the role of town crier for litter, low back fences and the worrying break-in at number 17. And last, but not least, let's forget how tame we usually are in the face of the opposite sex, and snuffle out as many rear ends as we can, quickly, while the dogs aren't looking.

Same adventures again tomorrow?

The Numbers And Letters Game

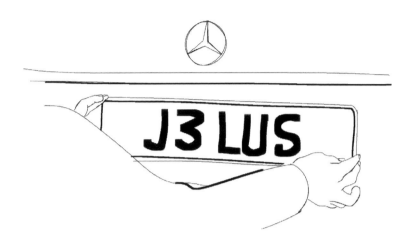

Look at that idiot over there in his Peugeot 206 with personalised number plate. What an absolute TO55 BAG and KN08 EDD! Excuse the vulgarity, but he started it …by wallowing in, what is, a misguided and misspelt self-importance and, embarrassingly, identifying himself as a three-inch wonder in the process.

If he thinks we're going to be wowed by his conspicuously naff brand of egomania and alphanumeric wizardry, which does nothing more than lift us from the crowd, attract lots of mainly favourable attention and make us feel good about ourselves, then he's got another thing coming.

Multiple offers.

Resolute Hoot

Wrong! Midnight on December 31st means it's resolutions o'clock.

Wrong! We expect to be congratulated (a lot) on our vague promise of commitment, before we've even begun committing to it.

Wrong! We have the willpower and patience to make it well past nine hours this time, providing we don't wake up any earlier.

Wrong! We're not setting ourselves impossible goals, such as avoiding all eye contact with biscuits and cakes.

Wrong! We're not easily discouraged or distracted. But why are Jaffa Cakes so cheap when obviously they're so yummy!?

Wrong! We're doing this because we want to do it, not because we're supposed to do it, we've been told.

Wrong! We've learnt from our previous experience of binging on Jaffa cakes when, at the time, we should've been doing sit ups, but accidents happen.

Wrong! We won't be too soft-centred on ourselves.

Wrong! We'll remember that, despite our orange jam-coloured skin, we're perfect anyway.

Wrong! We'll break down our daunting task into doable bitesize chunks, in spite of them easily being eaten whole.

Wrong! We'll cleverly turn not not eating Jaffa Cakes into a double negative positive habit.

Wrong! We're not scared or worried about reaching our goal because we know there'll always be chocolate digestives.

Happy New ~~box of Jaffa Cakes~~ Year!

Is That The Time?

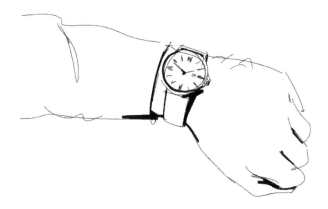

We're late*, We're late!*
For a very important date!
No time to say 'hello, goodbye'

…because some people's movements in life really aren't as valuable, or ticking along as nicely, as ours, and so, understandably, they might get a little wound up by that.

Also, we're type 'B' personalities – ballsy, blasé, blissfully bemused by Big Ben – which causes our inbuilt mechanism for appreciating both time and good manners to go wildly askew. Our sincere apologies for that. But we should be with you (type 'A' folk) in a few thousand years or so. If at all.

———————

*Again.

BUSINESS

Poo for the price of one

Thesaurus

buy, gloomy, Jellogg's, prettify, slated, hyperbole, indoctrination, transparent, monopoly, acquired, grotesque, hearsay, annul, sale, greed, suitable, pliable, sell, bollocks, incensed, guise, bazaar, bunk, divine

We Don't Like Change

Three coins in the fountain. The 1p, 2p and 5p. Thrown in with gay abandon – partly for luck, much like they are with arcade penny-pushing machines*, but mainly because the useless lumps of metal won't buy us anything for toffee anymore (or Black Jacks, Fruit Salads, etc.), which means they just end up clogging up our purses and now redundant sweet bowls.

Small change is still important to some people, however. Such as the penny-pinching councils of many a UK seaside town, whose coffers seem finely balanced upon us dispensing with it, like pennies from heaven, into their fiscal arcade machinery …and also to numismatists – more commonly known as successful penny-pushers.

---

*Which can be shoulder barged at will, depending if the coast is clear. It's worth noting that our luck, in both scenarios, is determined by how the coins land, plus, of course, in the case of the arcade machines, our shoulder mass.

79 Minutes To Obsolescence

The world's longest lasting light bulb was first switched on in 1901 and, amazingly, as of January 1, 2020 (today), is still going strong. Contrast this feat of human brightness with the bulbs above our heads right now – which, typically, last between 19:01 and 20:20* before succumbing to the darker side of modern life, and going pop.

Regrettably, the art of blatantly making goods that break or fail, seemingly after just 79 minutes of exiting their significantly longer lasting packaging, is just a product of innovation and unfettered capitalism.

Terribly dim of us, or watt.

_____

*In the evening.

No More Joca-Jola

Product placement.

For British TV and film producers, prior to 2011, these words meant only one thing – for the hair spray and make-up to be within easy reach of the main leads, please, darling.

But following an updated broadcasting ruling, our leads have now undergone a complete and utter transformation, without the need of John Frieda or VO5, into what appears to be screen-sized packs of Kellogg's Corn Flakes and Methuselah-sized bottles of Mountain Dew, all, of course, planted within convenient eyeshot of the main viewing audience.

Charming.

Getting Our Faking Airbrushed

Unfortunately, not all of us can spot the real person in a line-up of just two at magazine-reading length – of, for example, a woman who's been rudely awoken by the milkman after recently getting back from a two-day bender at a Caister Soul Weekender*, and an airbrushed advert of a spotless organism from Venus (otherwise known, according to the mag's editors, as the same person).

But then, in all truth, nobody's perfect.

---

*A long-running biannual music event, for people with real soul and character …and who are *definitely* not getting any prettier.

Iffy Shades Of Grey Spray

Why, Mr ambassador of automobiles, with the veritable rainbow of grey colours you generously park before our eyes you are really spoiling us. Mercury greys, Lunar greys, Meteorite greys* …such assortment of life-less lacklusterment is out of this world.

Because who on Earth would want to be seen in a captivating and exquisite – but highly depreciating – *red* Ferrari Rocher, right?

---

*All of which causes us to crash into each other a lot, partly because we have trouble distinguishing them from the hue of roads, but mainly to add some much needed colour into our lives.

Swerve The Corporate Curves

Attention startups and, largely, small business owners.

If you're storming over your new draft corporate logo then please refrain from any last minute urges to strategically blast forth a bananas-like curvaceous line anywhere within the same hemisphere as your precious brand name.

Unless you're Amazon, or Lazy-Arced Curves R Us, then these sweeping contour-like lines will not be interpreted as strokes of flair and vision – on the contrary, they'll be seen as symbols of abundant wind and hot air appearing on the horizon, as any well-rounded meteorologist will affirm.

Virgin On Harassment

Dear Virgin Media Occupier

You've been selected for a one-time offer of free advice.

For the past millennia or more you've been extracting my precious resources and using it, almost daily, to harass octogenarian Daphne – and everyone else in your area – with precipitous red propaganda pamphlets promoting your profane TV packages. Please will you prohibit any further use of such preposterous PR …you prize prats!

Make the switch today, and save yourself.

Yours caringly

Planet Earth

Pole Chancer

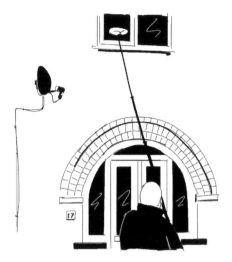

Want a well-paid outdoor job but don't like heights, hard manual labour or getting your hands dirty? Then try 21st century window cleaning, which involves none of the above – just you down below with a bucket load of ~~suds~~ takings and enough poles, hose and water to irrigate Africa …plus Ruislip.

Furthermore, because the bendy cleansers struggle to shift bird feathers, let alone their turds, you'll be finished in a jiff and soon vaulting over to your next little bonus job – with flexible and adaptable tools of the trades in toe – cleaning out the neighbouring chimney.

Controlled Printing Zone

With less ink than a traffic warden's pen*, printer ink cartridges are notoriously more expensive than both blood (PL-0713) and liquid gold (PL-0714).

Yes, whether we've just run out of something and we quickly need to pop in a new one, stopping work on double yellow lines can be a real pain, especially when we get caught by overzealous and corrupt corporates intent only on increasing their revenues, rather than simply letting the ink/motorist flow more freely.

Virtually deserving of a punch on the nozzle, whichever way we look at it.

---

*Either we're talking the nineties or someone's stolen their digital assistant.

Fruit And Pledge

Supermarkets deliver. Don't worry, though, they pick everything off the shelves with the utmost care and attention, like we do – and, *hopefully*, avoid outbreaks of all soiled goods like the plague.

Such as the exceedingly-plump chicken we once found relaxing in the vegan chocolate egg section over Easter*, before belatedly getting returned it to its more "natural" place. Or the boxes of tissues we witnessed getting sneezed on by a widespread number of contagious snot heads. Or the crusty-looking rolls ditched by the dry-skinned man with the itch. Or the apple and cucumber neatly shelved by the talented bat and ball pairing, on their way to field less active positions on the tills.

Every suspicion helps!

_____

*A whimsical, but downright dangerous, move.

Building Crocks

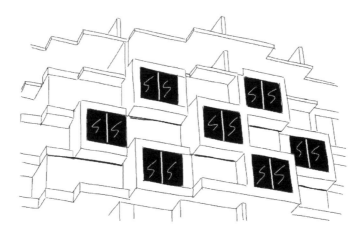

They say the greatness of a civilisation can be judged by the way it constructs its buildings. For example, Egyptian – majestic and strong, Greek – influential and enduring, Roman – powerful and empirical. Mayan – rich and sophisticated.

And then there's ours.

How do we accurately describe a hard-headed society whose prime real estate, typically, features featureless, flat-packed, fat-packed blocks, built quick in a trick brick stack, to make a big, thick, sick, stack?

Unsurprisingly, ever so easily – ugly and capitalism.

Trump FREED After Four Days Trapped Inside Metal Box!!!

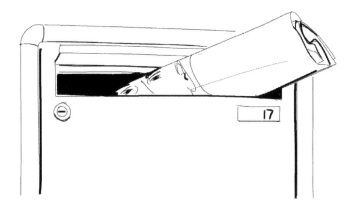

Headlines sell – and especially if we're in the newspaper or magazine industry. Or the Botox one.

Unfortunately, though, that hard fact is one of the few truths we'll find these days in an industry where, increasingly, yearnalists resort to reducing world events down to sensationalist-style gossip because it means an easy profit.

At least we can take solace in the only other solid fact in today's paper, which is that, tomorrow, Britain is set to SIZZLE in temperatures HOTTER than The Bahamas!!! (and the Sun).

The Great Cancel Scandal

No longer wish to entertain a TV package, or gone a bit cold on an energy provider? No problem. Have a chat with our Delhi department, which is dedicated to dealing with all levels of dissatisfaction and disgruntlement – right up to despair and disembowelment. Please have to hand the following:

- details of your account
- a fairly comprehensive grasp of Hindi
- three hours spare, plus an equally implausible amount of patience and civility
- a helmet, plus padding for walls
- a scalpel

…and we thought getting out of the EU was hard.

Now, let's see what we can do.

The Tills Are Alive With The Sound Of Musak

Has your brain been turned to mush by the constant bombardment of modern day marketing? Unable to control your urges when confronted by a crazy crazy wow 80% off price label, or by a gifted man of sales called Rich, or by the sneaky piped smell of bread and pies at your local oven shop?

Then, gather round, gather round. What you need is Brain Regain. Try it free for 30 days, or your old crusty stale brain back. No quibble. And did we say it's free-fitting Friday, so don't miss out and get your new brain here today – offer ends Tuesday*.

––––––––––

*Because you've shown a passing interest in a new brain, you might also like to buy a new hat to keep it warm and safe in.

Snacking Between Reels

A riddle, wrapped in a mystery, inside an enigma, masking a crime, tinged with comedy, of a heist, that's the horror show of snack prices at cinemas, theatres, sports events, etc.

Nachos and something that snot cheese – £6
Hot dog that's not hot and, one hopes, isn't dog either – £8
Pick 'n mix sweets – £2 per 100g. Interest-free credit available on filled bags.

While making extra-large proceeds on secondary products like these does make some sense, in that it helps to make ticket prices more affordable, to more people, the extra-charged proceedings does leave something of a sour taste in the mouth* and, unless we're super rich/stupid, gives us no option but to dive into our bulging handbags instead.

———————

*Not unlike those sweets and, worryingly, thinking about it, also that hot dog.

Only When It Suits You, Sir

With 90% of UK male office workers, nowadays, turning up to work without a suit and tie on, there's got to be a stitch up going on in the workplace. Undoubtedly, we've all seen top tech execs wearing the smart-casual ensemble – think thick-cloth jacket, atop crusty jeans and creased T-shirt – and so we've been fleeced into thinking that, by emulating them, we'll be automatically precipitated with the all-important smart part of that double-breasted cliché.

We need reminding of the positive psychological effects that dressing in a suit has, which contrasts sharply to dressing like a ragamuffin:

- Apart from village idiots, all suit wearers are perceived to be successful, powerful and a cut above; and
- Provided there isn't a snot-ridden hanky poking out of the pocket, they signal professionalism.

For these reasons, it's suggested that, with immediate effect, all office workers revert back to the more formal and traditional look. If only but on dress-up Fridays.

That'll Tauten Us

Looking to reverse the signs of trading, plump up profits and reduce the visibility of white lies? Then why not get the latest in scrote serums by Impossibollox.

Benefits: Specially formulated babble rejuvenates sagging bottom lines and improves the appearance of spin.

Usage directions: Apply liberally to all packaging and marketing, then rub in repeatedly, two or three times a week, into the minds of non-youthful people with droopy skin but firm bank balances.

Ingredients: Fake-scientific, cosmetic, wording, enriched with hyperbolic flaccid and a hapless celebrity endorsement, all blended to create redensified, unregulatoryfied, facial matter.

As foul as a baby's bottom, or our money back.

US Commercialism, By Will.i.am Fake

And dig those treats in insufficient time,
Stalk upon Englands abstains scene:
And was the Halloween that trod,
On Englands pleasant cultures seen!

And did the Impertinent Swine,
Shine profit upon our crowded tills?
And was US Commercialism builded here,
Among these dark Transatlantic Spills?

Bring me my Black Friday of yearning unfold:
Bring me my baby showers of aspire:
Bring me my Gear: All shrouds are sold!
Bring me my Shop riot buyer!

I will not cease from this Mental Sight,
Nor shall my Hoard sleep in my land:
Till we have unbuilt US Commercialism,
In England's green and with, currently, far too much American presence
Land.

Business Scarred

What's in a business name? Well, if we're starting up a new company in today's competitive market then there's likely to be a whole lot of irritating made up nonsense. Not least because most decent names have now been taken, but also because many startup owners have the creativity of wrecking balls, and can't spell for Toffifee.

Forget about company names which are just plain wrong, such as Crabby Dick's, Beaver Cleaners and Wally's Private Parts – we're talking about ones like Trivago, Zopa, Shpock and Opodo, all of which have no saving humour or irony, or, indeed, letters in the right places*. And I'm not making these names up by the way.

My advice to businesses, if I had to spell it out, would be to choose names that are short (*tick*), memorable (*tick*) and pulled from dictionaries, instead of Scrabble bags (*tick*). Note that, at the time of writing, Tick is available (*tick*).

---

*Or mention of genitalia.

Half Man Half Woman, By Cliché

In the commercial game of pong, it's the marketing demigods of the perfume advert who take on us coveting half-wits, who can't smell our arses from our elbows.

At half-speed, and in half-light, a half-naked lady appears, stepping half-consciously through half-ruins, and across a half-inch of water. With her mouth half half-open and half half-smiling, she beckons us in for a half-minute of visual half-truths. At this point, our trousers have, half-stupidly, slipped to half-mast, and we've become the butt of her half-jokes about the size of our half-grown, half-pipe. Half-drowning in embarrassment, we now half-remember what we came for – to pay *fully* through the nose for some half-arsed fragrance, and to half-heartedly head back to completely stale reality.

Nice Form, Shame About The Function

The famous old adage, 'form follows function', handily and, at the same time, beautifully, describes the notion that the function of an object should have priority over its appearance. Nonetheless, in today's ultra-modern world, we can consider that axiom axed – if not completely turned around and obsessively redesigned to within an inch of its practicable existence.

Because, if we're unable to sit on an attractive-looking chair for long because it's as comfortable as being whacked around the buttocks with a bat; or if we can't open a door easily because its slick and handsome handle was designed by a slippery knob; or if we're not able to season tonight's dinner as the groovy grinder is past its two-week lifespan – then we need to head straight back to the drawing board. One that, preferably, is made out of rock.

Craft Fear

As a nation of shoppers, it's unsettling to see so many of our high street shops going for a Burton. However, all hope's not lost quite yet, because not only do we still have the streets ahead Amazon for all our shopping needs but we also have, stepping up to the handmade plate, the 'street ahead closed for local craft fair' to make something out of too.

OK, these places may not be noted for their high-end merch* – in fact, some say they're just bazaar celebrations of local creativity, where elderly people slump asleep behind stalls, wrapped from head to toe in homemade blankets borrowed from the neighbouring stand, and where punters craftily keep safe distances at all times from welcoming beckons – but, then, where else are we going to go for all our uniquely cheesey, wonky, hangy, leathery, wickery, glittery, pottery, flowery, jammy, fudgy, soapy, cup cakey, homemade thingy needs?**

We'll think about it.

---

*Despite what the Harrods price-matched labels might indicate.
**eBay.

Cutting Edge Clocksuckers

Another day, another dollar.

Time to de-risk the problem of having eight hours of tedious work ahead of us by solutionising it with seven hours of timewasting, turd-polishing, corporate jargon:

- ✓ From the get-go, blue sky thinking about the weather, and our next holiday.
- ✓ Touching base with the mission critical loo, and circling back to it often.
- ✓ Bringing to the table our food chain snacks, fleshing out a grapefruit and trimming the fat off our bacon sandwiches.
- ✓ Being on the same page as the crossword, before game-changing to the more joined-up thinking of the dot-to-dot.
- ✓ Onboarding as many cups of tea (special sauce) as possible.
- ✓ Drilling down into Amazon to do our due diligence on our home deliverables.
- ✓ Gaining traction on our low-hanging fruit, while we've got wiggle room and no one's looking.

- ✓ Downsizing the little time we've got left by thinking outside the box of Google search, and pushing the envelope over to the neighbouring desk.
- ✓ Rowing back home, pivoting, getting into bed and pulling the plug.

Irregardless of all the dead wood speak, and pain points of the day, we very much look forward to buying into it all again tomorrow.

Crushed Lives

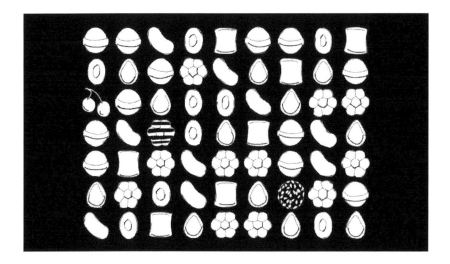

Doing nothing. The perfect antidote to the busyness of 21st century living, as recommended by science, Buddhism and the comedian Micky Flanagan, in his hugely hectic stand-up show, which, among other things, extolls the virtues of lying down and just staring at the ceiling*.

While most forms of reflective idleness, like this, are great for our personal growth and health, we can only wonder what Buddhists would say about our devotion to the mindless, but relaxing, cause of casual gaming. Day after day of thoughtful contemplation over coloured candy that, inexorably, leads to a path of liberation of, say, hard level 377, by paying millions (each day) to the creator for, hopefully, even more fruitful lives.

…probably, 'proper fucking nothing for brains.'

---

*A practice known as doing proper, old school, fuck all, according to the philosophical teachings of ~~Buddhism~~ Mr Flanagan.

TECH

Anyone got a screwdriver? …Hammer??

Thesaurus

artichoke, inaudible, battle, spin, extract, LOL, wrung, instrumental, shoot, strides, fingered, moustache, produce, juvenile, plastic, foreign, watery, habit, standstill, fake, kiss, box, play, antics

Going, Going, Con

In 2018, Christie's auction house sold an AI-created artwork of what looks to be a vague and rather rushed daubing of a fat-cheeked man with white paint around his neck, probably in the middle of wallpapering* ...for $432,500.

One computer science professor, who shall remain shameless, says some people nowadays are more inspired by machine art than human art. I suggest these are the same people who, when studied in much finer detail, couldn't hit a winning bidder with an auctioneer's hammer, let alone a cow's arse with a banjo.

---

*Dissatisfied with that lengthy title, the Paris-based computer creators went with *Portrait of Edmond Belamy*.

There T'annoy

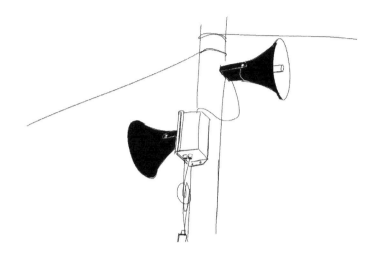

Platform 1, Platform 2 and Platform 3.

An example of three different destinations where public address (PA) systems would be priceless, if it wasn't for their confusing racket and pointlessness (CRAP) …where even the simplest announcement about the sudden and shocking state of the toilets is as clear as poop, and harder to unravel than a broken loo roll dispenser.

However, PA systems do have their uses, although none are necessarily listed on the back of the tin:

1. To scare birds away from getting too close, which is more humane than spikes.
2. To attempt to publicly apologise for their sound quality …the PA system's, not the birds'.
3. To advertise their whereabouts, via echo location, for their immediate disposal.

Data Moaning

We've forced ourselves to embark on a perilous journey across the choppy waters of phone channels, to liberate us from a dodgy, some say Hitleresque, data deal. Having previously carried out vital reconnaissance, the only thing now standing in our way, as we begin to launch our assault, is deciding on a plan.

Do we try to secure airwave superiority by going with a tied-in package – with inclusive minutes, texts, 15 gigs of data, some roaming destinations and a bit of entertainment and secure net thrown in – or, put up resistance, dig in, and go for something even more impossible to decode. It's a tough call.

One thing's for sure, though, if Churchill and Roosevelt's D-Day plans were half as complex then we wouldn't be speaking to each other at all.

Retreat!

Marty McCannotFly

This is heavy, Doc.

The bojo manufacturers of 2020 hoverboards are clearly experiencing technical "holdups" in the face of Earth's gravitational pull, which is causing them to have all the hovering power of a pregnant elephant.

Great numpties, Marty.

They've winged it by inventing a Trade Descriptions Act-defying why-botherboard of the past. But you've got to admire the bare-faced cheek – which, by the way, will be the sure-fire result of riding one.

Looks like where we're going, we gonna still need more roads.

Cleaning Up On Us Suckers

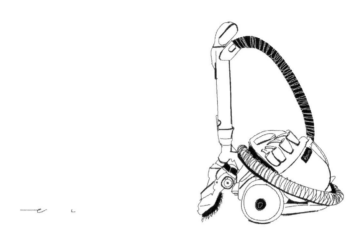

With designs by Ridley Scott, of *Alien* and *Body of Lies* fame, and Ego Boost as standard on all models, it's not hard to see how Dyson's range of Superchronic™ products have sucked us all in over recent years, and left their competition for cyclonic dust.

If only we could wave an actual magic wand to see through their patent-picking pomposity, hot air hype and over-engineered piles of ponderous plastic. Then hey presto. No more filth!

Unsafe Text Offenders Caught Trafficking

Having trouble keeping in touch with people, or achieving those arbitrarily difficult, but amazingly easy-to-remember, 10,000 steps a day? Then there's a single-step solution – become a petextrian, a walking texter, and you certainly won't look back.

Although looking like a dozy dumbass in a TV sketch for silly walks – tripping over curbs, face planting into lampposts* and continually getting in the way of cars – does have its negatives, it does enable us to rack up exactly one million steps, having, unavoidably, gone miles off course in our friends keepy-uppy process, and texted on a range of things, including @!*#? drivers who don't @!*#? look where the @!*#? they're going.

---

*Some of which, in more accident-prone streets, are equipped with protective padding. Other, less forgiving, places go for the much more measured spike option.

Ding–Ding–Diiiing

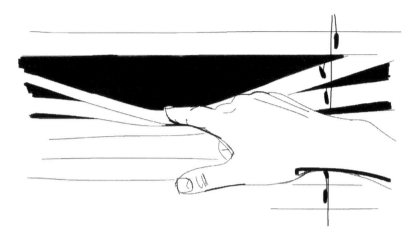

That's the sound of Amazon's till ringing each time we answer the store to spend £200 or more on one of their Ring doorbells. They're certainly seeing us coming, at present – from *all* angles.

But perhaps instead of overcomplicating our lives …and revealing to would-be burglars that we're at work right now, putting in a shift of over-time to pay for our doorbell, so please help yourself to the certain bounty of other expensive and superfluous goodies that lurk within …we should just stop answering the repeated, nuisance, calls of tech altogether.

That doesn't mean we shouldn't allow ourselves the odd peak now and then, through the curtains, but we just need to be a bit more watchful about what we open ourselves up to, that's all.

Sour Sour Music

Most of us don't mind a bit of computer in our music. Think Orbital, The Chemical Brothers and Clear History*. But it's now emerged that computers might soon be able to automate the song business in its entirety, Simon Cowell-like. Quick. Clear future!!

For sure, it's great when Spotify, or cheaper Russian music sites, use tech wizardry to recommend music to us – but when technology is used as the source and sound of the music itself, it becomes a threat not only to the music industry**, but to our innate ability to produce and appreciate art.

Mozart, et al., must be turning in their violin cases.

---

*Look it up, although they might have disappeared by now.
**Like cheaper Russian music sites.

Big Camera, Small Tripod

In a world where technology bestows upon us leaf-sized phones, bearing pip-sized cameras, what bygone lumberjack would want to be seen in public with a 60-year-old version of the latter, the size of the tree's trunk?

Broadcasters. We've all seen them – the Steadicam guy at the match, who somehow remains steadi despite having a circus bear attached to his midriff. Or his padded colleague on the halfway line, surveying the scene, and swivelling around, like he's captaining the Starship Enterprise. And then there's the warzone cameramen and women, instantly making themselves known to the enemy with their grenade-launcher-sized – and positioned, and aimed, and ready – camcorders.

Hopefully, in time, we'll fade out these macho-posturing, oversized, shooting weapons, and cut to using undersized, but equally sharp, smartphones instead. And looking at last night's highlight at the game, which made the news, where a cameraman (with accompanying bear) hilariously tripped over his seated colleague …we already are.

Broken Motion

Automatic doors.

In spite of the infrared passive and active Doppler radar approach sensors, tuned to 10.5 GHz, combined with secondary back-up infrared monitors, light beams from every which angle and pressure-mat sensors to monitor our every movement – the truth is that we're still inconvenienced by the inevitable need to break our stride on final, on final approach to them.

At least with old school flappy doors, with happy handles, we could plan ahead.

Dopamine, Manipulate, Repeat

Every time we use social media, we are being *buy* manipulated into *our new* doing something that *ridiculously-named* we would never *ointment* normally do.

No, that doesn't mean wishing aunt Maudie a lovely a time at the doctors (re her embarrassing piles), it means getting surreptitiously abused by algorithms into changing our behaviour, according to the wishes of paying customers of the likes of Facebook *you gullible bunch of Anusols*.

Trembling Etch-A Sketches

In 2016, a Dutch company unveiled, *The Next Rembrandt*, a computer generated painting that apparently "brings the Master back to life". Note that, like in almost all of Remmie's works, the subject is a white male, 30-40 years old, bearing bumfluff, a hat and a family-sized floppy dinner plate around his neck. Plus facing to the right.

The company said they spent 18 months using advanced technology to predict what the artist might have painted next. Going by his clear penchant for oblique white men in hats, my old Commodore 64 could have foreseen the same thing in just two days, while simultaneously running, and jumping, Daley Thompson's Decathlon in the background.

Steves' Labours Lost

Shiny, healthy and tasty one minute – wrinkled, gone off and worm-ridden the next. If we compare Apple Inc. to its fruity, and actually good-for-us, namesake then its steady decline has been inevitable – not least because there's no amount of packaging or pesky slides that can forever hold back nature. So welcome to Steves' fruit stall, specialising in, what were once, *exceedingly* select Apples:

- The Product Launch: crunch time, quite juicy but delivering a superficial taste.
- The iPhone: everyday favourite, despite average flavour every day.
- The Apple Watch: tart, untimely and uncooked early-season variety, so should not be consumed.
- The Arrogance: self-styled golden suspicious type, rich thick skin but acidic taste.
- The Tax Avoidance: disease ridden, and full of holes with maggots squirming around inside.

Apple. *Think deference.*

Go Back To Old Kent Road

Children, see if you can spot the difference:

a) A kindergarten, on casual bring-a-toy Friday.
b) A newsagent's pick 'n mix counter (by the comics).
c) The selection of games available in app stores.

Correct. There's no difference because, it seems, they're all monopolised by smiley-faced and sweet-toothed toddlers, under the age of about five – with the glaring exception of The Beano and the chocolate tools, in particular the scrumdiddlyumptious and, more importantly, *long* handsaw.

App developers. Pay a £10 fine, or take a "chance" with adults.

Breathe In, Read Out

Speaking spontaneously without the need to recite our words through a transparent, yet, ironically, acutely visible, A4 glass autocue feed.

Hmm!? We never see driving instructors gawping cross-eyed through such cheat screens when declaring to us the virtues of speed limits. Or policemen doing ditto when issuing us with speeding tickets – or, indeed, solicitors when skilfully getting us off. So why do business and political leaders, the very people who we'd expect to be out in front when it comes to being articulate, if not above the law, feel it a requirement of the job? *pause for applause*

I have a dream that one day leaders of our nations will budge on the colour of their spin and especially on the content of their teleprompter.

This Voice Needs Deparrrrrrr-ting

Heathrow Airport. The welcome mat of our country. Cadbury's choc-full of the best of British to invite us all in with, with virtual life-sized posters of Buckingham Palace, a rolling green countryside and a long-time stationary (and grey) Stonehenge. But this is Britain. So let's not start to feel too welcome, just yet.

'A-tten-tion. Weel a-ll parssen-jaars pleee-se go twoo Gayte twent-ee furve.'

Wrong. The announcer hasn't just come back from the dentists, and we haven't landed in Amsterdam or Newcastle by mistake, either. We've indeed arrived at Britain's favourite airport announcement control centre, where a new artificial voice system called AvioVox has landed ahead of us – a system that, 'operates in more than 24 languages*, makes announcements in perfect English, and sounds just like you and me.'

So that's 100% tone deaf and Dutch then …just like the manufacturer.

---

*So that makes it at least 25.

Too Amazon By Half

Despite being the world's biggest company, Amazon are surely getting too big for their roots to last. The great shopping "river" may have huge volume, but its profits are a puddle and, arguably, it has way too much needless packaging in its basket, which may need to be edited if it's to continue to checkout successfully.

Review items

Cardboard boxes, books, retail, health care, finance, electronics, web services, groceries, tickets, travel, music, video, art, publishing, TV and movie studios, etc. totalling about 40 different "tributaries".

Payment method

It seems likely that the company will soon flood the world for everything, but other businesses are getting wise to this and unless it starts to convert its massive flow into larger pools of profit, it will eventually stagnate.

On that basis, Amazon, would you like to continue shopping, proceed to checkout, or remove some items from your basket?

Phone Checks And Imbalances

Tic. Tic. Tic. Tic. Tic

That's the regular/irregular reverberation of our brains beating them-selves to pulps, as they pump out essential hormones to our eyes* and thumbs*, so we can check our phones for the 3,600th time this hour**.

Oh. Still no Likes of that picture of us looking down expectantly at our phone. Let's *see* if we've been bequeathed anything instead, or been made king/queen of Monaco overnight. Actual important notification just in! A man's at the door saying that our mum *Dee*, who's terribly ill in hospital and on a drip feed (like us), is in low power mode (and, no doubt, soon to be in sleep mode) and that we need to come right away. With her charger. And vine loads of grapes.

---

*The most important, and expressive, organs of the body.
**In fact, we check them so regularly that we can set our clocks by it. By going to Settings, then General, then Date & Time.

Stop Gap

In an effort to save thousands of lives, speed limiting technology looks set to be introduced on all new cars sold in Europe from 2022. Contrast this restriction to the ability of the EU itself, whose drive to apparently curtail progress remains, as ever, unlimited.

Perhaps also then, in an effort to save lifetimes of needless waiting around at traffic lights …while staring longingly at the other side, and into the temporary tranquillity of chequered boxes, especially when nobody else is around …we should limit their use altogether, and go red/amber, then green, on the idea of just using our eyes, ears and common sense instead.

Or just get a bloody move on with self-driving cars will you!

Ickbait

Picture the scene.

A colossal cruise ship is out to sea, and heading straight for a sinkhole that's too unbelievably big and swirly for words (but not pictures). Surely, the captain must be in a right old spin – but no – he's seen these kinds of far-fetched images tonnes of times before on websites like YouTube, and knows from experience that clicking on them, like a demented dolphin, will only reveal the depths that the sinkhole providers sink to to satisfy our shallow curiosity.

It turns out that the captain was right. The sinkhole was just a large shoal of inquisitive fish, lured in by what looked like an improbably massive, bloated and dead blue whale afloat above them …with lemming-like figures plopping into the water beside, and gaseous bubbles coming out of its stern.

Lip Reading

Lips. A useful part of our faces, found right under our noses*. Pre 2005, their main function was considered to be for eating and speaking, but, with the rise of selfies, it turns out that for piles of us they have an even *more* vital bodily role – that of pouting in photos, like clenched arseholes.

The purpose of the pucker is not, as one might reasonably reason, to display our affection for latest social trends or lipstick shades, but to demonstrate our vanity in the face of the ugly truth that we can't all be good looking …hence, the pressing need to squish our lips together in a cheeky (slash psychotic) attempt to disguise our underlying awfulness.

XX

---

*Assuming our heads aren't tilted (for added effect).

Pop Up Circus

Pardon me for being so rude.

It was not me, it was my greedy, and crude, marketing department.

It just popped up to say hello, and now – with the touch of a wilfully obscure, almost invisible, in fact, cross symbol – it's gone back down below.

It's just like going shopping on the high street, isn't it? We pop in to Tesco to have a browse of their cheap range of pork pies and spam, and, immediately, having scrolled down the aisle no further than the welcome mat, we're accosted by a pop up clown asking for our inside leg measurement. No thank you, we say, but by all means have the length of our outstretched fisted arm instead*.

---

*Usually aimed top right if we want a knockout blow.

2020 Poor Vision

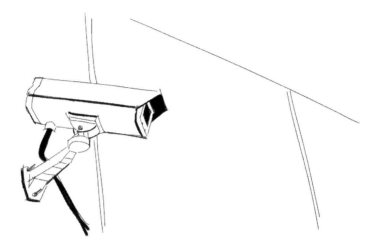

Assuming we haven't been on Mars for the past 30 years, and that we don't have vision and memory problems, then we couldn't have failed to have seen, and recorded, how much of our everyday lives these days are being filmed.

Worried? Well, we absolutely shouldn't be, because the 2020 reality is that unless we're only interested in stealing video doorbells or door mats, then the CC*TV cameras we're likely to face are merely going to be cheaply run deterrents, which – upon clear close up – can't tell the difference between an unearthly, orange-looking, creature** and a fuzzy, cheesy, puffed-up, puff*** …neither of which have any hope of standing up in court.

Nothing to see here.

---

*Completely criminal.

**An unmistakable description of an alien, not Donald Trump.

***An unmistakable description of Donald Trump, not an alien.

Still Lives

These are not just any old ants, these are ants photographed and filmed in the *process* of being any old ants, which, according to us, makes them very special any old ants indeed. But the ants needn't all get ahead of themselves.

Because camera phone operators like us – otherwise known as soldiers, as we're never idle with them and we've got gigantic heads – take, and then harvest, commonplace images like these all the time in anticipation that our work might one day get the approval of some big superorganism, or, failing that, to simply remind us of the memory*.

Sadly, though, this is a mistaken, collective, labour of love that needs treading on firmly, if not certainly reducing down to more single files.

---

*Should our much more focussed, and better at recalling, brains be later removed.

W⊘RLD & SCIENCE

With great knowledge comes great irresponsibility

Thesaurus

English, odyssey, backdate, caveman, toast, stinks, timber, fogginess, path, jingle, sensitive, sick, patriotism, barriers, finite, contaminated, extreme, unspeakable, sluggish, retrograde, hardened, whetted, sendoff, waste, suspicious, bias, overhaul, tramps, decorated, rascal, orientation, Stevenage, disturbing, open, departure

An Americanism/s Problem

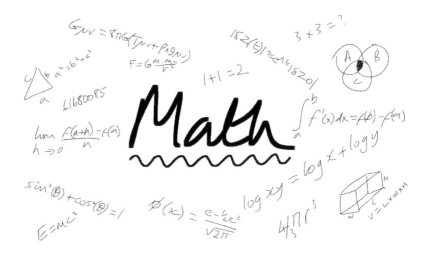

Math is so difficult isn't it.

Not only have we got a fraction under a zillion numbers to contend with but we've also got a squillion, squiggly-looking, symbols to struggle with too ~ in particular, the (red) one (shown above, in a black red) that, quite correctly, appears under the word "Math" to indicate a basic ~~typo~~ spelling mistake – see me after class!

By curious contrast, the not unrelated words and subjects, "stats, physics and economics", all seem to be much easier to understand and to say for our American cousins, and so with these we can just minus off the red squiggly line and add a great big ~~check mark~~ tick.

Lots Of Small Steps Of Man

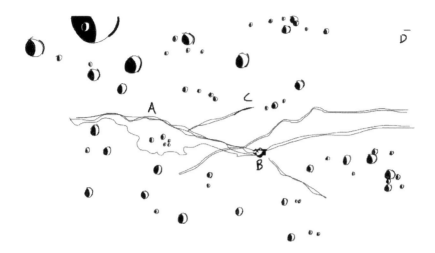

If you've ever doubted man's footstepping on the Moon then take a look at this 2009 overhead image by a NASA orbiter (recreated in drawing form*), as also detected by Chinese, Japanese and Indian spacecraft.

The wiggly tracks 'A' you can see were probably not made by a family of mice scurrying around over a big fatty lump of Swiss cheese. The landing module 'B' is unlikely to be a running wheel to burn off excess cheese. And, in all likelihood, the flag 'C' is not the mice's earlier cheese-stained washing hanging out to dry. You copy?

---

*So not to scale, or 100% guaranteed to be like the real thing.

Note: Mark 'D' denotes an unerringly straight finger slip, and not a large black, Kubrick-like, monolith.

Backs Under The USSR*

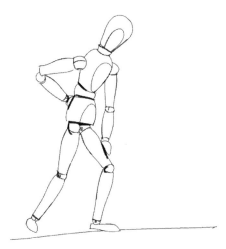

If, as seems likely, future evolution bestows upon us bigger thumbs, necessary for better massages, and to grab hold of ever-expanding phones and chocolate bars, then one hopes our backs won't be left behind in the melee.

Because, in the short time that we've walked on all twos to free up our hands, our spines have been through more physical stress and unnatural posing than Ronaldo on match day – who, give him his due, is always first to acknowledge to the crowd the far more important role his back plays in his goals than his head or feet.

---

*Utmost Strain Since *(the rise of)* Running.

Transporting Eggs In A Vice

In spite of the warnings, most of us hunters still wittingly carry our hard-earned gatherings in a material that's inherently lethal to life, over the short to extremely long term.

OK, they may be handier than a hand, but our use of poisonous plastic bags to simply shuffle stuff from one cave to the next is as naive and reckless as popping out for a juicy lump of red meat knowing that it's Brian's* first day on the till.

Therefore, the next person found miscarrying like this will be given a gag for life, i.e. they will quickly have it placed over their heads, and then tied down …as in the bag, not the (equally effective) carnivorous mammal.

---

*The incredibly hungry and huntery sabre-toothed tiger.

Global Warming Nonconforming

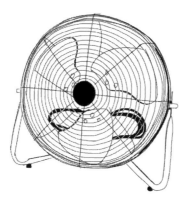

As the totally annihilating but, for now, quite pleasant indeed, thank you, asteroid of global warming continues to hurtle straight for our bronzed heads, we're all under instruction to give it a big collective blow now and then to cool things down, and to help change our course.

Under no circumstances is any couldn't care less, half-hearted, blowing allowed – from anyone! Naturally, when we say anyone, that doesn't include Presidents, Prime Ministers, heads of state, business leaders or asthma sufferers, all of whom have provided hand-written notes from their mums and/or shareholders, and so are excused from this important lesson.

Smell My Breeze

Asthma sufferers and those allergic to having their DNA mutated and lungs neutralised by wrecking Reckitt's* cans o'chemicals – you might want to look away now, and have a pre-puff.

I've just sprayed some "Evening Meadow at Dawn" Pre-Poo spray down the loo, then I'm going to squeeze out more of the nasty whiff in the afternoon to bequeath the entire house, and ultimately beyond, a complete death of fresh air. Enjoy!

---

*The manufacturers of Pre-Poo, as well as many other frightfully shite sprays.

Real Treetops Glisten

Now children, listen. If your holidays are to be merry and bright this year then your Christmas tree, like good old Santa Claus himself, has got to be *real*, not fake.

Because, contrary to popular myth, cutting Douglas Spruce down in his pine fir just a few weeks of festive bauble dangling is actually great tidings for the environment* – unlike those artificial plastic rotters**, which are pure make believe and, unfortunately, just like the ones I used to know.

And may all your Christmas trees be right.

———————————

*Without them, for example, there'd be 100 million fewer trees growing in the UK, with all the benefits they offer. Plus, Santa says so, or no presents.
**That don't rot.

I See Clouds Of Grey, Blue Skies Too...

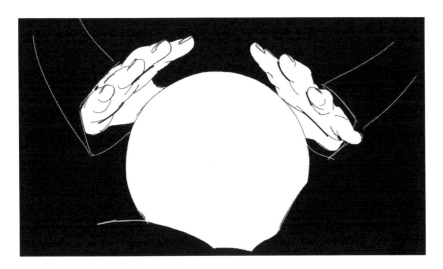

...because I'm a long-range weather forecaster, so not got a Scooby Doo if truth be known.

Yep, if we thought today's apples are not at all like yesterday's prediction of oranges then we 'aint seen nothing yet. Try peering much further into the future life of our chaotic spinning orb, with the help of a more time-travelled oracle of weather, and it won't be single fruits anticipated to fall on our heads, it'll be the whole basket.

At least aunt Maudie is going to come in to some money.

Horse-Drawn Miscarriage

After 150 years of leaving Horse-Drawn Carriage Street, take a left-field direction onto the now clogged AD2020. Keep left. Caution: graphic traffic ahead, trying rerouting. We are on the fastest route. Road, clearly, doesn't work ahead, try making a U-turn. Turning the clock back is denied. Continue on the cruel carriageway then for another 200 yards, or until we break down from old age, whichever comes first, then, at the roundabout, take the fourth exit.

Turn right, turn right, turn right, turn right.

Welcome back to Horse-Drawn Carriage Street. We have reached our predictable destination, which, without 2020 foresight, is, rather idiotically, the place from whence we came.

Tally-ho.

Broken Slogans

There now follows excerpts from, *British Election Messages Since the Seventies.* A fine read indeed. It can usually be found under romantic humour. If not, try fairy tales.

'*Labour Isn't Working,*' says The Iron Lady, with straightened face. But Margaret, '*The Labour Way is the Better Way,*' retorts a discontented but still sunny Jim. You two should '*Go Liberal,*' adds David, with customary steel. '*The Next Moves Forward,*' commands Maggie, from right of midfield. Mags boyo, '*Britain will win with Labour,*' isn't it, replies (Welsh) Neil, with newfound confidence, and much found balance.

Major announcement, '*New Labour, New Danger*'. Hmm, don't you mean, '*New Labour, New Life for Britain,*' challenges an energetic and honest-looking minor. '*Strong and Stable,*' affirms Mrs Maybe, after sliding a beer mat under her lectern. Talking of which, counters Jezza, beer must be '*For the Many, not the few*' …and hence they all lived happily ever after.

N.B. Boris Johnson is somehow managing to '*Get Brexit Done*' despite his hugely disadvantageous position of being dead in that ditch.

Allergic Non-Action

Having read recently about a woman who has a genuine allergy to cold weather, my immediate reaction was equally sincere (and bitter). It's January in England for folk sake – stick a jumper on like the rest of us and, providing you haven't also got allergies to tarmac and quinoa, head south by foot, which will soon warm you up. But then it dawned on me.

What we're witnessing here is not just another example of feeble people stupidly biting down on latest allergy trends – it's all down to our messed up immune systems, brought on by our inescapably-sanitised western lifestyles. Doubtless, the best advice is to revolt – to get dirty a lot more by abstaining from using soap and all other household cleaning products.

Or to just remain up north*.

_____

*Sorry, that was cold and unnecessary.

Cancer Of The Govainments And Pharmacoupticals

Assuming I've got a readership of one, not including me, then, statistically speaking, you or I will definitely get cancer at some point in our lives. Heads I win, persistent headaches (or use of my dodgy double-sided coin) you lose*.

But if it wasn't for the long-term malaise of global government funding into the disease, and the even sicker state of major pharmaceutical companies, whose practices *inhibit* the creativity and risk-taking needed to achieve breakthroughs, then we'd both be winners, regardless of what's spinning around in our heads.

---

*I don't smoke, I still play sport regularly (chess, which gets surprisingly sweaty with the heating on) and I eat porridge with blueberries twice a day.

The Rise And Fool Of Nationalism

It's back! Sadly, not the Football World Cup, but the equally goal-oriented and futile exercise of nationalism, which comes around every four World Cups or so.

Here's today's line-up:

1. **Germany**: safe pair of hands in recent decades, but now letting in far too many.
2. **Russia**: tough, uncompromising defender, prone to own goals but often effective in attack.
3. **Saudi Arabia**: skilled at zonal defending and man marking, good in sudden-death situations.
4. **Italy** (c): confident and on the ball, strong tackler and blocker, adept at playing the dummy.
5. **Turkey**: fired up again after a stint out of the game, solid at heading off challenges.
6. **Japan**: compact utility player, liable to letting the odd ball fly over their heads.
7. **Austria**: not the authority of old, but has real power going forward.

8. **France**: free spirit and good at passing, liable to playing a few too many stepovers.
9. **Hungary**: fans' favourite, right winger, solid shielder of play.
10. **Britain**: target man, looking to take on the world after recent Euros exit.
11. **USA**: playmaker, currently extremely selfish in front of goal.

Subs: India, Poland, Philippines, etc.

Today's mascot: North Korea
Referee: Us
Attendance: 7,600,000,000

Signs Aren't Good

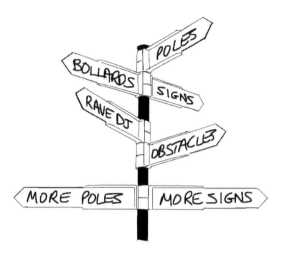

If we go down to the shops today
We're sure of a big surprise…

No, not that we'll find no shops (at the time of writing) – the bombshell is that there isn't any room for us, what with all the bollock-high bollards, signage and poles* in our way.

Yes, Britain's high streets are deserted, of the human kind, not because of online shopping or squeezed incomes, but because we can't get ourselves through to the shops for the obstacle course of street furniture and superfluous notices, which do nothing more than point us in the direction of the bleeding obvious and the nearest exit …oh, and also, thankfully, last month's rave event.

---

*Of the upstanding, dedicated and hardworking *metal* kind.

Puzzling Slow Boat To Angina

2 Across: The one thing that disproves the adage that all good things come to those who wait (6)*

1 Down: Bad spell for elderly lady, *anagram* (7)**

Fitting indeed. If only the more cryptic clue as to why we grow old at all was as easy to answer. Experts put our inexorable ageing and fragility down 2 a lifetime of breathing in poisonous oxygen, which, rather absurdly, slowly kills our bodies. God!, gravity and plain greed, respectively, are thought to be to blame for other, perhaps even more mysterious, things – such as the misplacing of our keys and joints (as in hips not drugs, although they're never where they should be, either), our droopy boobs and our comforting, but increasingly worrying, dependence on bingo and sherry.

---

*Old age.
**Granmaa.

City Blights

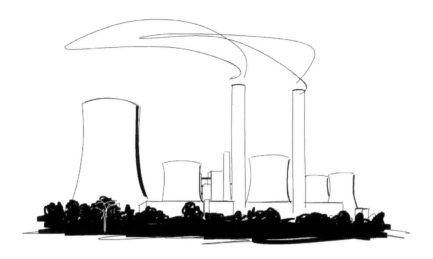

In most big cities today, the number one sight isn't, as we might think, a gravity-challenging monument, an oversized hamster wheel or a grandiose building for politicians to spin around in. It's sulphate and black carbon. Also known as gravity-challenged pea soup. More commonly known as smog.

And with nine out of ten of us breathing in the stuff, which is so corrosive that it turns lungs black and Taj Mahals green, isn't it about time that common sense took over, and for communities to counter it by convening all us common folk in comfy coffeehouses by the coast? …before we all end up with a collective coronary, and in *cough*, in *cough*, in *cough*. In boxes for dead people.

Three Steps To The Start

Step 1

In the beginning, when science was just a glint in God's eye, man's first crack at understanding the night's sky, and his place in it, thoughtfully concluded that it must all be the work of a supernatural being, in a big white coat.

Step 2

In spite of countless scientific beings in lesser white coats proving otherwise, man holds on to the belief that the man in the big coat is still most likely to account for all the smaller beings in coats.

Step 3

Man who's fanatical and adamant about the supernatural appears, without a coat on at all, typically in a long black get-up, throwing abuse and much, much, worse at wearers of all sizes, and most denominations, of coats.

Oh, God!

Step 1

Speak Wow Or Forever Hold Your Peace

The human voice box. If you've never seen it in action, then be warned! It's more repulsive and alien-looking than the very alien-looking alien in the film *Predator*, which is about aliens. Hence, this might explain why so many of our accents are – and to quote in Mr Schwarzenegger's dulcet tones – such ugly movverfuckers.

Nothing against the Dutch, for example, but the only thing missing in Dutch's* weaponry from the film, was a namesake Dutch accent. Surely, with one of those in his arsenal it would've triggered more long-term damage to the alien's ears and morale than any fancy rifle could. And, taking this logic to its logical conclusion, if only the leading man was named Texan, Brummie or Essex – the alien would've just surrendered on the spot!

---

*AKA Arnie**.
**AKA accent man.

Ice Cream For Dessert, With Long Flake

Our bodies may be the most advanced things in the known universe, but there's one area where, bluntly, they're as undercooked as primordial soup.

That rawness is the lethargy and sleepiness we tend to feel after eating, whose effects, bizarrely, are the opposite of what we might expect from an energy refuelling process …rather inconvenient, for example, if we still happened to be cavemen and women, whose happy meals, unhappily, are miles from the safety of our caves.

The gut feeling of science is that this tiredness is caused by the energy needed to break down food, plus our natural tendency towards fatigue at around two am/pm (triggered by brain chemicals). Put less politely, and scientifically, my gut feeling is the human body remains a trifle sloppy, and still has a half-baked sponge for brains – so best if we leave it for another 30 mins* or so.

---

*Millenniums.

The Feeble Has Stranded

When I was young, men were walking, driving and hitting golf balls on the moon*. 50 years on, and it's not a telescope we need to see how far space travel has progressed – it's, yes, you spotted it, a microscope.

Commentary on the descent stage of man and Apollo leaden

CAPCOM   Humans. You're go for stranding. Over.

Feeble   Roger, understand. Go for stranding.

CAPCOM   Feeble looking great. You're go.

Feeble   Picking up from Musk. 30 feet, 2 and a half down. Faint shadow of hope, shifting to the contrite a little.

CAPCOM   30 seconds.

Feeble   Drifting alright. Contact light. Okay, engine stop. Humans, Undesirability base here. The Feeble has stranded.

CAPCOM   Roger, Undesirability. We copy you on the ground. You got a bunch of guys about to turn few. We're leaving again.

From the moon, I should add. It is, of course, impossible to whack a golf ball 240,000 miles …even back in those days.

Sm⊗ther E⊘rth

Pave. Tarmac. Concrete. Asphalt. Patio. Gravel. Cement. Tile. Cobble. Instructions for use:

1. Find an area of natural, treasured, earth. For example, Mr Smith at number 17 wants to replace a square metre of grass in his garden with concrete, as a place to store his grass seed and mower.
2. Lay the hard, scabby, blot on the landscape, taking care to fully choke the ground habitat of any water, air and nutrients. Don't worry about entombing, forever, little, lost and hungry baby moles* and insects.
3. Also, don't worry about its terribly drab looks (the concrete's), or laying the foundations to flooding and irrigation problems, trapping unwanted gases, the bio-diversity crisis, air pollution, respiratory issues and total and utter environmental degradation. Or it causing bloody mayhem with our feet.
4. Clean tools, which can be found in the token square metre of grass we left untouched, and head for pastures new, should there be any – which there won't.

---

*Who are also cute and blind.

Water Babies

Contrary to grown-up thinking, our unquenchable thirst for bottled water has nothing to do with well-lubricated multinationals, and their greed to pacify us with murky reinventions on a pre-existing, cloudy, theme. Nor does it have much to do with our body's desperate need for hydration.

No. It's because we're all needy, attention-seeking, cry-babies who can't find taps on our own, and so default to sucking on plastic dummy substitutes instead – despite them costing the earth*, and yielding less nutrition and more bacteria than the real thing.

What huge dispensing tits we are*.

---

*In both senses of the phrase.

Americano, With No Phoney Sweetener, Please

So long, farewell, auf Wiedersehen, adieu and g'night.

As parting expressions go, all of these do the job fine – even the oddly spelt ones, because pleasantries spleasantries. And I could've even added a primitive-sounding "grunt" to the list, but for the difficulty of its spelling, which, from experience, and for all we care, would've also done the job OK.

However, adding 'have a good day'* to the mix is where the niceties must end, at least for us Brits. Because who, for example, at a quarter to mid-night at the petrol station, wants to hear such robotic nonsense, uttered with utter disregard to sincerity, and to the time of day**. Thank goodness the warmth of the farewell, and the distinct lack thereof, was certainly not matched by the coffee. Bye.

---

*A derivation of 'have a nice day', typically recited by millennials in service positions, who often struggle with hellos too.

**One assumes that if they were referring to the (just) 15 minutes left of today then the phrase is *doubly* pointless …and unpleasant.

Litter Of Apology

Dear Planet Earth

We'd just like to say how sorry we are for being a lazy-arsed, throwaway, society, that can't help chucking used baked bean flavour crisp packets out of car windows, plus other random shit, then blaming the resultant mess on non-biodegradable packaging and bad wind. We realise that you aren't our dumping ground, and that we shouldn't be casually turning streets, roads, the countryside, rivers, coasts, oceans, animals and our-selves into hazardous conveyors of litter like this.

You must be angry, and rightly so – we are utter rubbish and should pay the penalty. You have several large active volcanos at your disposal that could be used for recycling, or if you can't be bothered with that then there's got to be an empty field somewhere just begging for garbage to be emptied into it.

Yours, getting rather worried now

Potato Head

Positive Negativity

Page after page of moaning about life and being critical about stuff. Who needs this harmful* negativity in their life?

At first frown, being continually irritated by things might seem to be a dire choice to live one's life by, and for a book – but the role that being a cowardly cynic has played throughout history, and in our ultimate success, should not be criticised. Circular wheels didn't just roll into existence on their own, they required many hours of poisonous pessimism, savage scepticism and sick cynicism to provoke others into getting the job done**.

Like it or not, being negative is here to stay because it's the rock upon which society both grows and expels its natural gas, much lichen breaking wind. This is evident by the number of books bought on the subject, as seen on, say, Amazon, which shows it sitting neatly right up there between cooking and yoga – an exceedingly tasty position, in anyone's book.

---

*Yet entertaining.
**No Kwik Fit or Halfords in those days.

Favoured Flavours

Life's not fair, and it's not dark either. It's a mix of all colours – as well as ethnicities, genders, ages and classes. It's an Earth-sized box of chocolates and, fortunately, unlike the film, it comes with a helpful description card, so we know exactly what we're going to get.

If, for whatever customary social reason, certain flavours are considered unequal and harder to swallow then 1) tough toffee, and 2) we need to change our tastes, because the box doesn't exist at all without everyone, of every description, in it – and neither do we.

Humans. *Always the finest ingredients.*

Do not throw to the dogs.

Life In The Farce Lane

Earth-shattering quake strikes America ...*three days*. Meteor-sized hole sinks Japan ...*two days*. Puny pothole pricks England ...*five years* (if fast-tracked). These are the times taken by the respective countries to repair damaged roads in the wake of the stated devastation.

Yes – where, in England, we suffer from occasional drizzle, and a permanent work ethic that, rather gloomily, revolves around worker speed limits, red tape, whining, head scratching, indiscipline, fence erectile dysfunction and fag breaks – other nations endure real, calamitous, hold ups, but just get on with the repairs. No lateness, no fuss, no reading of dirty mags on the hard shoulder (or soft verge).

Highways England, you have been warned – end of minimum speed, and no more waiting or stopping at any time ...unless, naturally, it's in amazement at the likes of the Americans and Japanese.

In Need Of Change

'Need cash for vital drugs research'
'My Jag needs a new wine cooler'
'Lost all my money on the 2.30 at Aintree – my wallet must've fallen out my breeches over one of the jumps or something. But I did win the race again, so not all bad!'

If these whimsical cardboard signs are anything to go by then beggars haven't got much to worry about – they'll soon get a job in advertising, or on *Have I Got News For You*. However, most struggle to extract much humour from their position*, understandably so, or indeed much money, contrary to popular misbelief.

The fact is the vast majority of beggars come second in life through nothing more than sheer bad luck, so let's cool down with the whining shall we, and stop sneezing on them like the stereotypically squalid society that we are.

God bless you.

---

*Seated on hard pavement, in all weathers and, seemingly, way below us.

Scheming Of A White Christmas

Christmas. A time for excessive gift giving, travelling, lighting up and farting* …and, possibly, combinations thereof. Unfortunately, the consequence of all this is that there's extra chart-warning carbon in the atmosphere, at this time of year, rather than heart-warming snow.

To counter this, perhaps if we could stomach moving the dates (and sprouts, etc.) on a few months, say, to Easter time, then we'd have a much better chance that the folkloric tradition will come down upon us and, albeit holy inappropriate, resurrect, what is seen by many as, the true spirit of Christmas.

---

*Caused by a general loosening of inhibitions – plus an overloading of dates and sprouts.

Rogue Sanctions

After months of slaving away, we've managed to build ourselves a nice little wicked and corrupt country, which deprives its citizens and turns us into messiahs/very naughty boys. If we wish to continue to see our system of rule survive then please decide which of the following we'd most like to see imposed upon us, without delay:

a) International sanctions – causing further suffering, hardship and seclusion, plus a large villainous smirk, and little finger to the mouth.
b) Military action – as per a), but with even bigger grin, and both little fingers this time.
c) Diplomacy and constructive engagement – causing noticeably loose bowels.

Clue, definitely not c) stupid. Now shoo.

Navigating Everyone's Secret Weakness

A helpful little reminder there that, for one in six adults, we still have difficulty quickly distinguishing our left from our right, and so need a little direction*. Consider the 'N' and 'S' compass points in the mnemonic to be a bonus because, by contrast, absolutely nobody has problems with north and south – not even Kim Jong-un.

Weirdly, though, while the majority of us can instinctively tell our left nostril from our right finger, everybody seems to struggle with 'east' versus 'west'. But that, of course, shouldn't come as too much of a surprise …given their respective directions.

---

*If we've forgotten which side of our brain the mnemonic is stored in, or we're in a rush, then we can simply make an 'L' shape with the thumb and index finger of each hand. The one that looks like an L is the left.

Inviting Stevenage

Stevenage, the town I grew up in, invites us to attend its 75th birthday on 11th November 2021. Having suffered with ill health over recent years, through no fault of its own, plus poor press, as in badly worded, our attendance would be much appreciated.

How to get there
Super accessible by train, plane, car and bike. Boats, less so.

Things to look out for
Like most 75 year olds who've worked hard all their lives, and with little help from the government, it's looking as though it could do with a big win on the bingo. First up then, bang on the drum, 71 – beautiful countryside, dedicated cycle paths, 19 minutes from London (by train, not boat), historical New Town, even more historical Old Town.

Did we know?
25% of the world's telecom satellites are made there, as is Europe's first Mars planetary rover. To infinitely great Stevenage and (not) beyond!

RSVP (Rejuvenate Stevenage's Vast Potential).

Lacking In The Mental Department

Plotting our way through life is as much a mental struggle as it is a physical one. Crock a leg in this game and it's a quick trip* to A&E. But drop a peg in the brain, as it were, and it's a slow suffering slog to E&A ...as in Eternity and Awaiting.

That's because, while more of us are now coming forward with our mental health problems, like the mature adults we are, the appropriate services in most countries are, by contrast, still holding back on their clear deficiencies up top. Fortunately for us, this is nothing that a weekly gathering round in circles for an unhurried and painful leg crocking won't help to resolve.

---

*Hilariously, this being the cause of many a crock.

Whether Phenomenon

So, the rotating whirlwind of childhood is gone, and the force of nature that once enabled us to speak our minds at will, to the joy of the flat sea of grownup restraint, has almost fizzled out.

Sadly, for most of us, adulthood signals this sea change in the whether – that is, whether, in the face of twisted maturity, we should continue to be outspoken, knowing full well that it's now likely to result in turbulence, not pleasure, and only going to appeal to those who've continued to remain true to themselves.

Of course, this narrows the field down to the tremendously bold, honest, energetic, happy, charismatic, successful, empowered and powerful among us – of which, unsurprisingly, or should that be surprisingly, there are so few.

Another Nice Mess

And finally, it's with much sadness and regret that we announce the death of the great veteran double act, Earth and humans. After a relatively short bout of illness, Earth* succumbed to a combination of factors brought on by humans**. These included numerous acts of exploitation – such as kicks to the backside and twists of the nose – which, although rather enjoyable at the time, came to a tipping point (like a piano on a flight of steps) that, inevitably, led to its downfall.

Amusingly, Earth's final words were 'why don't you do something to help me?', to which humans could only respond with a trademark tie twiddle of embarrassment and look of disgust to camera. *Classic!* Unfortunately, as is common with long-time double acts when one half passes away, it's unlikely that the other half will last much longer now …or have anywhere near as much fun.

The End

---

*The thin one.
**The fat one.

BY THE SAME AUTHOR

16-page work with big words, as mentioned earlier, which the author suddenly remembers was about a young kid embarking on an exciting journey to explore and understand the world, armed with just a bean bag and triangle. SPOILER ALERT – after a long journey (47 years and 217 pages) the boy achieves his goals.

Watch this space, eh. (that's a friendly request, not another book title)

INDEX

TEN TOPICS THAT DIDN'T QUITE MAKE IT

1. The ridiculously expensive price of Frazzles at my local corner shop
2. China
3. Loan sharks (*'Daphne, it's for you.'*)
4. Facebook
5. Annoying kids being annoying by doing annoying wheelies down the street, and making me wonder if I could still do that (the wheelie part)
6. Attention seekers at work
7. Donald Trump and Vladimir Putin (would've been a single, united, topic)
8. Aggressive driving (*'Are you c*** or someting?'*)
9. The death penalty
10. The lack of any hint of synchronisation between fireworks and music, typically, when the former are set to the latter. Surely, with just a few calculations of the speed of light relative to that of sound, plus wind variables on the night, this is avoidable.

***unt.

TH✪SE ⊠ETAILE⊠ N✪TES

As recovered from my lost and then found (obviously) phone:

- Find out whether 17 pages counts as a book these days.
- Quickly register the internet domain imeanitdaphne.com before some-one else snaps it up.
- Pants is a funny word, try to squeeze it in.
- Check for overuse of highly unnecessary, and very, very superfluous padding words – unless they're deemed 150% useful.
- Have a last minute rummage* through to try to add Boris Johnson and his hair in somewhere, for effect, even if it means messing it all up**.
- Shit! – what if people reading *this* still haven't laughed much lately?
- Desperately need porridge and loo roll.
- Google how to get past level 377 on Candy Crush.

---

*A repugnant word.
**A repugnant habit (that of messing one's hair up for effect).

OTHER EXTREMELY ELABORATE ATTEMPTS BY ME TO APPEAR BUSY

- Plundering the picturesque back bedroom (in more than one dwelling) for the purpose of producing slightly unsightly art.
- Spending exactly a hundred years trying to build Tick.com (with my brother Anthony) – 'an online platform that presents definitive public opinion on virtually everything' – and then, eventually, being woken up.
- Learning to proofread, which, before you highlight anythng, was a clear error.
- Chancing my arm at buying and selling internet domains, such as spinspinspin.com, which, I've now realised, is even more frustrating than gambling on the slots.
- Playing chess constantly when I should've been strategising about the 'king state of the back garden.
- Studying the piano for six months, after which time my playing style became a fusion of Elton John and Lang Lang – namely John Laing, the company who makes a racket digging up roads.
- Working on an idea for a ~~second~~ third book!

The following pages are for emergency use only …such as when you lose your phone and need to make a load of notes, or when you're caught with your trousers/skirt down in a poorly serviced train station loo, in which case you'll find the ending to this book to be not only truly, *truly* satisfying but also a real life-saver.

NOTES

NOTES

NOTES

Printed in Poland
by Amazon Fulfillment
Poland Sp. z o.o., Wrocław

54348394R00148